I0752660

THE PATHWAY TO THE SACRED HEART OF JESUS

FR. ROBERT I. BRADLEY, S.J.

THE PATHWAY TO THE SACRED HEART OF JESUS

A RULE OF LIFE

Edited by Betty B. Bosarge, O.S.F.

Angelico Press

First published in the USA
by Angelico Press 2026

For information, address:
Angelico Press, Ltd.
169 Monitor St.
Brooklyn, NY 11222
www.angelicopress.com

ppr 979-8-89280-195-9
cloth 979-8-89280-196-6
ebook 979-8-89280-197-3

Book and cover design
by Michael Schrauzer

CONTENTS

PREFACE

FATHER ROBERT IGNATIUS BRADLEY (1924–2013), S.J., in his life as a priest for 58 years, often said that he had the *cor animarum*, the care of souls, as his main responsibility, even though he spent the majority of his priestly life as a scholar and professor, first of British history and then theology and catechetics. But like St. Thomas Aquinas referring to his work in writing the *Summa Theologica* as "straw," Fr. Bradley said that his main goal, his number-one priority, was to teach Catholics of all ages how to surrender themselves to God to do His holy will, and show them how to plant their feet solidly on the narrow, rocky pathway that leads to Heaven.

He wanted everyone to find their way to the Sacred Heart of Jesus, to enter into the Sacred Heart, and there find a taste of Heaven here on earth. With the help of our Blessed Mother and St. Joseph, he taught that this is truly possible and the perfect way to live because we are all part of the Holy Family. By living within the Sacred Heart now on our earthly journey, we will find ourselves in the arms of Jesus and our Mother Mary upon our natural deaths, he explained. How could it be otherwise?

Named after St. Robert Bellarmine and St. Ignatius Loyola, Fr. Bradley by age three knew he would become a priest. He studied diligently, always with his head buried in a book, and became fluent in Latin so that he could follow his older brothers and serve daily Mass for Bishop Charles White in the Diocese of Spokane, where the Bradley brothers—four future priests—had what they called "the franchise" to serve the bishop's daily Masses at his residence. And it was a battle to see which two brothers fulfilled the task on any given day, as Bishop White's mother, who lived with him, was a skilled baker of pastries and cakes which were always offered to the altar boys after Mass. The future Fr. Bradley was the bishop's favorite altar boy, as he had the most perfect Latin, such that his brothers teased they had to teach him English as a second language.

As a high school student at Gonzaga Prep in Spokane, the young future priest pursued his quest for finding out how we could live within Jesus' Sacred Heart here and now. He didn't want to wait for Heaven. He thought there must be a way we could get into Jesus' Heart and find tremendous love there here on earth. This devotion to the Sacred Heart was fostered by his love for the Blessed Mother, who was showing him the way to her Son with the three Rosaries he would pray daily.

Helping him too in his quest were his parents, Joseph and Muriel Bradley, who gathered the large family each night to pray the Rosary and read Scripture. There were the Jesuit priests and brothers at Gonzaga Prep who nurtured his vocation along with Bishop White, encouraging him in his mission of finding out exactly how we can live in the Sacred Heart here on earth in order to make a smooth transition to eternal life in Heaven.

After his ordination in 1955 in Louvain, Belgium, he began telling people there was a pathway to Heaven and that pathway flows from and leads to the Sacred Heart of Jesus. As he described it, the pathway is narrow, strewn with rocks, crevices and cliffs, and occasional avalanches of boulders and ice, with grizzly bears and mountain goats who would attempt to shove us off the pathway to our deaths.

But we must trudge on up the pathway. There is no "middle way." The only other way we can travel through life here on earth is on the twelve-lane expressway that leads to Hell. To paraphrase Jesus, choose the road to your final destination—Heaven or Hell—because He does not want us to be lukewarm, just hot or cold. Don't try to meander down the two-lane country road where you pick and choose what *you* like to do and what tenets of the Faith *you* want to practice, disregarding what the Church teaches, paying attention to God on Sundays by attending Mass and then mostly forgetting Him the rest of the week. *Jesus wants you all-in* for your journey here on earth as you head for your final destination with Him.

As Fr. Bradley was forming his thesis on how to find our way into the Sacred Heart, he spent much time in prayer, daily Mass, adoration in front of the Tabernacle, Rosaries, and memorizing many litanies in Latin to the Sacred Heart, the Blessed Mother, St. Joseph, and various saints. By the time he entered the Jesuit novitiate in June 1941, he knew the answer.

It is the *Holy Eucharist* that is the *pathway* to living within the Sacred Heart of Jesus, for true devotion to the Eucharist leads us to unite ourselves with Jesus, to give ourselves totally to Him, surrendering our will to Him daily, doing His holy will for us at all times, no matter whether our vocation is to the priesthood, religious life, or the laity. We are all called the same to live a life of holiness. We cannot delegate our prayers to the cloistered nuns or monks just because they may have more time than we have to pray.

As a Jesuit novice, Fr. Bradley began to formulate a way to teach the thousands of souls he would encounter as a priest how to get on the pathway that leads to Heaven. He knew he must catechize with every sermon and homily, explaining the Holy Eucharist to everyone who approached him with questions. He also realized he must write about the Holy Eucharist and the Sacred Heart to reach even more souls.

Thus, this book came to be over the years of his priesthood from his writings, sermons, homilies, retreat talks, and conference presentations. Chapter One includes an essay he wrote in 1943 in the Jesuit novitiate. Over 35 years as chaplain/spiritual director for Catholics United for the Faith, he conducted many retreats with the main topic almost always centered on the Holy Eucharist. He wrote articles for Catholic magazines, *Homiletic and Pastoral Review* for the clergy, and books, also contributing chapters for books written by other priests. In his years as a graduate school and seminary professor of theology and catechetics, he taught many classes on the sacraments, with the lessons centered around the Eucharist.

Fr. Bradley spent several years developing a Rule of Life for the Laity as a guidepost on the pathway to living within the Sacred Heart. This came about because when he was teaching a class or giving a sermon on the need to live within the

Sacred Heart, students and parishioners would ask: "Father, how do we get there?"

He realized it is a long and difficult journey to "get there," but one which he believed we should all attempt. Thus, he formulated the Rule of Life in three stages: Beginner, Mid-Level, and Living Within the Sacred Heart. It's similar to the three stages of the spiritual life.

His three brothers who were priests would tease him and told him he was a dreamer like Joseph, the son of Jacob in the Old Testament, when he told them he was devoting his life to leading people to live within the Sacred Heart. Was he a dreamer? No! It is possible to do what he explained and described—Jesus is waiting for each one of us and His Heart is wide open to receive us. We just have to make the journey, as rough and tough as it may be at times.

The journey is not easy. It often takes many years of trudging along to get there to the Sacred Heart, where we can rest deep within the love Our Lord has for us. Many of us struggle to free ourselves from worldliness and attachments. But the Church has provided many tools to help us in this struggle. There are the Holy Scriptures, especially the New Testament, the sacraments, the Rosary and the Divine Mercy Chaplet, the daily Liturgy of the Hours to give us inspiration and help from the saints who have gone before us, the Magisterium of the Church which teaches us the doctrines established by Christ and the early Church Fathers, and our good priests, religious, and fellow Catholics who will help guide us on our way and foster our growth in our spiritual lives.

Yes, it is a struggle, but one day we will know when we are reaching the pinnacle, the entrance into the Sacred Heart where we can dwell in peace and joy here in this messy and sinful world we live in. Over the course of our journey, God will help us lose interest in many things—good things like hobbies, music, TV, sports—that consumed our time, only to replace these things with better things. We will find ourselves being a helper to many others, with the Holy Spirit leading them into a deeper relationship with Jesus, His Mother, and the saints dwelling in the Church Triumphant.

Our lives will have changed for the better. There will be joy. We will find peace of soul. We will no longer find ourselves falling into despair or depression or, when sickness strikes, yelling out, "Why me, Lord?" We will be able to accept what God allows for us with total peace of heart and soul.

It will be a new life we have, a better way of living here on earth, for all who climb that narrow pathway to the Sacred Heart of Jesus. For He will be with you, holding your hand, filling you with His love for you every minute of your life. *You will never be alone!*

Come on the journey! It is like being halfway here on earth and halfway in Heaven every minute of the day. Be not afraid!

H*ow This Book Unfolds:* Fr. Bradley, in his typical professorial way, blends theology, doctrine, Church history, spirituality, and practicality in his writing. There are eleven chapters, with an Introduction to becoming one with Christ, followed by four chapters on the Holy Eucharist. Next comes a chapter on interior renewal, followed by penance. Because pursuing life within the Sacred Heart of Jesus is a goal that will trigger the enemy of us all, the evil one, there will be much suffering on the journey; to help us, Father has written about salvific suffering, which is followed by a chapter on the Sacred Heart. The final two chapters are on the Rule of Life for the Laity. A section of resources for further study concludes the book.

May this book help you obtain many blessings and the grace you need on this journey to eternal life in Heaven!

Dr. Betty Bosarge, O. S. F.
Editor for Fr. Bradley
May 2026

CHAPTER ONE

BECOMING ONE WITH CHRIST

"The Kingdom of Heaven is like a king who made a marriage feast for his son" (*Mt:* 22:2).

WHEN OUR LORD ON THAT HOLY WEEK evening spoke this parable, He knew He was walking to His death. He had already spent His last vain efforts to win over His enemies. Now that he had failed, His Sacred Heart, all but broken by the rejection, looked out down the centuries and across the continents. He would answer that rejection by winning all those other souls to Himself. He would make sure of it by buying them, and the price would be His life.

But the actual truth is that Christ did not think of it only then. The truth is that the salvation of all men was God's intention from all eternity. Why had He created man in the first place, if it was not because man, every man born into this world, is destined one day to live forever with God, his Creator? This is the great underlying meaning of the parable: that the marriage feast is the eternal marriage feast in Heaven; of Christ, the Divine Bridegroom, and the Church, His Spouse, which, as the embodiment of the human race, is destined to bring to the embrace of Christ all the sons of men.

That is why Holy Church is called "Catholic," because she is universal, offering the salvation that Christ has merited for all men, to men of every age, of every country, of every race, of every disposition of soul. She breaks down all the barriers of human prejudice and formality, for her universality embraces all, our enemies across the seas, as well as the poor, downtrodden people of our own country, the rich of good will, as well as the poor of spirit, "the lame, the maimed, the blind" at our own door steps, as well as those on the foreign mission fields. And she embraces the sin-weary prodigals of the world, the saints of repentance, as well as the little children, the earthly companions of the angels. It is to all that the invitation is given, that the House of the King, God's House in Heaven, may be filled.

But there is that other side to the parable which Our Lord took great pains to make clear to us. That is, that all, as a matter of fact, will not be saved. Not that all were not invited, but that all did not accept the invitation. And even among those who did accept the invitation, there was one, Judas Iscariot, who was cast forth into exterior darkness, where there is weeping and gnashing of teeth.

This means that, though God extends His invitation to all without exception, for Christ merited salvation for all men, still each one must give his own personal account of his use of those merits. For, as St. Augustine puts it, "God, Who created you and merited your salvation without your consent, will not effect your salvation without your consent." Here, then, is a matter for yourself alone. None, not even the all-powerful God, can save you, if you do not wish to be saved.

Do you realize this? If you save your souls, everything is saved. But if you lose your souls, you lose everything. Everything, because besides losing yourselves, you lose God, and that forever. That future life, in which you will never die, is determined by this present life which will end with your death.

Your one great desire in this present life, therefore, can only be and must be: You must save your immortal soul! Now, how are you to do that? By fulfilling the condition God has laid down for salvation, namely: that you love God and serve Him with all your heart. But how best to do this? Among all the means leading to this end, which is the one preeminent means? It is the frequent reception of Holy Communion.

It is our surest means for two reasons. First, It contains, or rather, It is, Our Lord Himself. What surer way is there to share in the Marriage Feast of Heaven, than to begin it here on earth? What surer way is there to be united with Christ, the Divine Bridegroom, than to be united with Him now in Holy Communion?

And the second reason is, that since we are united with Christ in Holy Communion, we receive a pledge of the perfect, unlimited joy of Heaven, of which this present marriage feast is the prelude, because you will possess in Heaven the same Jesus Whom you possess now, Jesus—God and Man.

Because He is God, He desires your salvation, since that is why He made you and became man for you. Again, because He is God, He is able to save you, since all that you must have in order to be saved is His grace, the grace given to us through His Sacred Humanity, the superabundant grace of His sacraments.

But you ask: "How will this sacramental grace of Holy Communion be sufficient for us in our daily lives? There are so many obstacles keeping us from loving and serving God with all our hearts." Dear friends, in comparison with the inexhaustible graces contained in Holy Communion, every obstacle to our salvation disappears. Let us consider our three great obstacles, each in turn.

First, there is the World, that is, the temporal things to which our nature is so necessarily bound. We have to work so much of the day for our food, clothing, and shelter. And there are our social duties, as fathers and mothers, employers and employees, sons and daughters, teachers and students, priests and parishioners. To so many a man and a woman this is the whole substance and concern of their lives. But for us who daily receive Him Who is the Fullness of Life, we realize that in seeking first the Kingdom of God, all these things of the world will be added unto us.

Second, there is the devil, Satan, who as our principal enemy constantly appeals to our passions, and through the occasions of sin, so often overpowers our sense of values. What should we do when these temptations come? Go to

Our Lord in Holy Communion! He understands your case perfectly, for He too had His temptations. And with Him in our hearts, we can speak with His strength: "Begone, Satan!" For blackness cannot remain where there is fullness of Light.

But what of the third and greatest obstacle, the Flesh? We cannot get away from ourselves; and if Christ will force no one to be saved, how can we overcome the fact of our weakness, that discouraging weakness of will, which faces alone such great tests of strength? It is overcome by that other fact, that Our Lord has so arranged it, that by our receiving Him in Holy Communion, we become one with Him. By receiving Him often, we become more and more like Him, until, in a certain sense, we will in time cease to be: we lose ourselves! And with us, all our weakness in the face of temptations, and all our too solicitous dependence on mere temporal things because for now, the soul, united with Jesus, is one with Him.

That is the one great fact of Holy Communion: we become one with Christ. In this union the past, if darkened by sin, is forgotten. The bright future is sealed, and the present, the living present, is all-in-all.

Make that present moment always present by the frequent reception of Holy Communion. The obstacles on our side—we saw that Our Lord has already removed them. And on His side, He is here just for us, and for each of us personally. By receiving Him often, we will save our souls.

There is the invitation before you. Will you accept it? Others have not accepted it, but you—Our Lord is asking for your answer.

You can refuse Him, just as others have refused Him. But really now, can you? In view of that eternal life to come, can you neglect this surest means to salvation? In view of the desire that you have for a full life here on earth, can you miss this Banquet, where there is served the Bread of Life?

In view of your own selves, all that you are and have, can you forget to return a thank you to the God by Whom alone you live, and move, and are? That God is here, our Jesus, our Divine Bridegroom.

In view of Him, of all that He is and has, even if He would invite you to share His Chalice also, as He invited James and John, can we refuse? No! We can accept! We can do anything for Him, even if it is to be bloody martyrdom. Why? Because we love Him, because His Love impels us, and we can be saved.

Indeed! We can be saints, giving our all to receive His all, poured out for us from His opened Sacred Heart, and waiting for us now in Holy Communion and to live within His Sacred Heart.

It is our Faith, our hope, the call of the Bridegroom, the call to the marriage feast. You can come. Jesus is here. Will you?

FAITH, HOPE, AND LOVE

In your journey to live with Jesus in His most Sacred Heart as you seek holiness and eternal life in Heaven, the theological virtue of *hope* guides you on your path. Knowing and living what Jesus taught us—His doctrines—is the reason for our hope. He very clearly told us what we must do to achieve eternal life, and the Apostles handed these guidelines on to us through the New Testament and the Teaching Church.

Despite all the troubles in the world and in the Church itself, hope is still there, isn't it? In fact, is it not the presence of these obstacles—not their absence—which defines hope? What is really at issue, then (and it is only because of these all-too-evident obstacles that we are forced to take note of it), is not so much whether we have hope, as rather whether we have reason to hope.

What is the staying power of our hope? What are its grounds? There is a reason for this hope of ours. And what is that reason? Ultimately, simply, and all sufficiently there is but one reason. Our hope is grounded on but one reality: the reality of Christ's doctrine, known and lived. And what is Christ's doctrine, known and lived but our *faith*? The only reason, then, why we have hope is that we have faith.

This explicit linkage between hope and faith, which is a linkage between effect and cause, brings to mind a classic statement which can well serve as the framework for our own growth in faith and our work in helping the Holy Spirit lead souls to Jesus. It comes from St. Augustine, that classic purveyor of classic statements, in his little treatise on catechetics entitled *De Catechizandis Rudibus*.

St. Augustine was addressing a young deacon who had asked him for advice on how to carry out his new job as a director of religious education. In response, the great Bishop of Hippo made this summary comment on the purpose and plan of religious teaching: "... so give all your instructions that he to whom you speak by hearing may believe, and by believing may hope, and by hoping may love" (*De Cat. Rud.*, chap. 4, no. 8).

What we have here, as summarizing the dynamics of catechesis as taught by St. Augustine, is a linkage of the three theological virtues, *faith, hope, and charity*, in the same sequence that St. Paul originally gave them (1 Cor 13:13). If we really understand these three virtues and how they are linked together, we will understand—as much as we can understand what is ultimately a mystery—*God's total plan for our life*. For these three virtues as linked form a lifeline from the beginning of our life of grace on earth to its final fulfillment in Heaven.

The causal connection between faith and "hearing" what Jesus taught us can begin, appropriately enough, with the phrase "the Profession of Faith that comes to us from the Apostles." This phrase (which echoes the English translation of a passage in our Roman Canon of the Mass) suggests two parts: the first part is the *source* of our faith, i.e., how our faith is linked to God. The second part is the *transmission* of our faith, i.e., how our faith is linked to us. And combining the two parts in the middle is the word *Apostolic*.

"The Apostles": what a vision comes before us with the mere mention of this name! *Gloriosus Apostolorum chorus* ("The glorious choir of Apostles"), as sung of in the *Te Deum*, the men whom Our Lord made as one with Himself as He was one with the Father! Their words were His words, no more nor less. When we hear them, we hear Him (Lk 10:16).

Indeed, Christ chose to have no other words than theirs. We might not have known His very existence in history but for them! Their words are those of *witness*: telling us what they saw and heard and handled—of the Word of Life (1 Jn 1:1).

These words of the Apostles were obviously *human* words, just as the words of the Word-made-flesh were human words. Yet at the same time the Apostles were totally certain that their human words as officially witnessing Christ were also His words and therefore were also *divine*. St. Paul so informed his Thessalonians: "We also thank God constantly for this, that when you received the word of God which you heard from us, you accepted it not as the word of men but as what it really is, the word of God, which is at work in you believers" (1 Thess 2:13).

THE DEPOSIT OF FAITH

These words of the Apostles, encompassing as they do all that they "received, whether from the lips of Christ, from His way of life and His works, or whether they had learned it at the prompting of the Holy Spirit" (as *Dei Verbum*, no. 7, put it), constitute what is called *the Deposit of Faith*. This is that timeless content of divine truth which is for all mankind its only access to the eternal life, namely, the one true God and Jesus Christ Whom He has sent (Jn 17:3).

Now in the Apostolic words which make up this Deposit of Faith we distinguish two forms or modes of their existence: they are either written or unwritten. They were all originally spoken words, for that was according to both the example and the mandate of Christ. The distinction between the written and the unwritten is therefore relatively unimportant. What is important is that all the words of the Apostles *as Apostles* are fully and equally human and divine.

Yet the fact that *some* of the words of *some* of the Apostles were committed to writing is significant. For in this form they continue the tradition of the Old Testament as something written. The written Apostolic words constitute "Sacred Scripture" as the New Testament, and as such occupy a most privileged position in the total Tradition called the Deposit of Faith.

With the Deposit of Faith thus defined, we have the essential component of the *source* of our faith. For here—and here alone—is God's revelation to man. Man's reception of the revelation—which we call faith—thus finds in the Deposit of Faith its linkage with God.

We can turn now to the second and more detailed part: how is the faith, once "deposited," *transmitted* to us?

How have we, following all the generations before us right back to the Apostles, received that Apostolic word—and therefore the Faith? As that word was originally the spoken word, so primarily it is by *hearing* that it is received. *Fides ex auditu* (Rom 10:17). There is also, of course, the *unspoken* word that is also heard—in the depths of the heart where the Holy Spirit moves the soul to recognize Divinity in the human words spoken. But, following the logic of the Logos-made-flesh, the interior (or subjective) act of faith normally follows upon the exterior (or objective) statement of faith made by those who hold the Apostolic office of witness: the bishops of the Catholic Church, the successors of the Apostles.

FROM THE APOSTLES TO THE MAGISTERIUM

Through nearly two millennia, the Apostolic Succession has made possible the transmission of the Faith, i.e., the contact with the timeless Deposit of Faith. This transmission has been effected primarily in the same manner in which the source was effected, namely, the living words of the bishops have followed the living words of the Apostles.

But, just as the written word was used by the Apostles to secure a privileged status in the Deposit, so too the written word has never been neglected by their successors, and that written word has also secured a certain privileged status in the transmission of the Faith. I am referring, first of all, to those declarations or definitions whereby the Church has, from time to time across the centuries, made solemn judgments about various things pertaining to the Deposit. This is the exercise of that office called the Magisterium. But this, please note, is not its *ordinary* exercise: this is the so-called "extraordinary Magisterium." What precedes and follows and wholly surrounds the Extraordinary is, of course, the Ordinary Magisterium.

Now the Ordinary Magisterium has also used the written word, and in fact this use goes back to the time when the Deposit of Faith was completed at the death of the last Apostle. As far back as the first century we can trace in some written form that "word" which in antiquity and authority is just this side of the Sacred Scripture itself, namely the Apostles' Creed.

The title by which this most venerable statement of the Faith has been known is thoroughly appropriate. For it has always been seen by the Church as the summary of her Apostolic Faith and is therefore her "rule of Faith" *par excellence*. Which is its more valuable attribute: its *completeness* or its *succinctness*? Taken together, these two attributes make it the perfect vehicle of the Church's profession and teaching of her Faith. For here is "the Faith, the whole Faith, and nothing but the Faith."

There were, of course, other written words used in that form of Ordinary Magisterium which in the course of the second century began to take recognizable shape as the Church's way of transmitting her faith. Besides the Apostles' Creed, two other fixed statements were being used in what was called the "catechumenate" (that primitive institutionalization of the "catechesis" or teaching of the Faith) as the very core of its curriculum.

These two other formulas were actually Scriptural: they were simply lifted out of their respective books in the Old and New Testaments. The Ten Commandments, taken from Exodus (20:2–17), or Deuteronomy (5:6–21), and the Our Father, taken from St. Matthew (6:9–13), were placed alongside the Apostles' Creed, which was the summary of the entire Scriptures.

Thus, as the bishops of the early Church began to structure her "catechesis," i.e., the formation of her new children in baptism, they patterned their ministry of the Word after the Apostolic ministry of the Word: like the Apostles their words were both written and spoken—written sparingly, spoken profusely.

Their written words, echoing the inspired writings of the Apostles, were, as it were, the core of the teaching: the Creed, the Commandments, the Our Father. Then, summarizing this core—explaining it, applying it, exhorting to it—were their spoken words: the "living" words which, by the help of the Holy Spirit in the hearts of their hearers, transmitted the Faith.

So far, regarding the transmission of the Faith to us from its Apostolic source, we are still back in the second century! How can we briefly get from that far-distant past to where we are now, nearly two millennia later? We can cross this immense span of time actually quite neatly. The first and briefest way of all is simply to invoke that historical reality called the "Apostolic Succession." Objectively, our Faith now is the same as the Faith then. That is to say, just as sure in its linkage as the *source of our Faith* is, thanks to the Apostolic Commission, is the *transmission of our Faith*, thanks to the Apostolic Succession.

But, since this transmission has been primarily by means of that most ordinary and universal mode of the Ordinary and Universal Magisterium, namely, by means of the *catechesis*, we should offer as briefly as possible a resume of what, happily, we can call "classic catechesis." This we can do by noting just four "moments" in this two-thousand-year span of time.

The first moment to be singled out in the history of the classic catechesis occurred when for the first time the catechumenate, already several hundred years old, got a concise and comprehensive formulation. So obvious once it was written—since it explained so aptly what had been taught so successfully—this formulation came from the pen of St. Augustine. In his *Enchiridion* (which he wrote some twenty years after his *De Catechizandis Rudibus*), he sketches the simple alignment which structures the classic catechesis, and justifies its timeless validity. By a stroke of genius he took the three fundamental formulas of the catechesis—the Apostles' Creed, the Our Father, and the Ten Commandments—and aligned them with the three virtues enumerated by St. Paul. The Creed teaches us what we are to believe, the Our Father teaches us how to hope, and the Commandments teach us how to love.

ST. THOMAS AQUINAS AND THE SACRAMENTS

The nicely compact triad of "creed-cult-code" is, however, not complete in itself. To make it organically one, to bring it to life and keep it there, something more is required: a fourth component. This fourth component did not have to be added as something extrinsic to the catechetical curriculum: in fact, it was because it was already there that the curriculum existed in the first place! The catechumenate, you must remember, was essentially ordered to baptism. It was the anticipation of baptism, then, which *formed*—which *enlivened*—the catechumens, and which therefore gave finality and efficacy to the catechesis.

The fourth component, therefore, which completes the triad of Creed, Commandments, and Prayer—and completed them not by some accretion from without but by a definite vivification from within—was baptism, and (by implication) the sacraments as such.

Some 850 years later, at the height of medieval Christendom, the great Patristic contribution to catechetics made by St. Augustine was to be matched and perfected by the Scholastic contribution to catechetics made by St. Thomas Aquinas. St. Thomas accepted totally the classic catechesis bequeathed to the Church by St. Augustine: and well he should have, for it had proved its worth as the Church's one indefectible instrument of transmitting the Faith—surviving the demise of the ancient catechumenate and creating "Christendom" in its stead.

St. Thomas' contribution consisted essentially in his development of that fourth catechetical component: the sacraments. The contemplation and study of the sacraments had developed well beyond the seminal intuitions of Augustine:

the "septenarium" was now a matter of defined Faith, and sacramental causality was now a prime object of theology. St. Thomas saw the whole economy of salvation as a sacramental economy. This centrality—this totality—of the sacraments in the realm of faith justified—indeed necessitated—its centrality and totality in the realm of catechesis, the teaching of the Faith.

But what St. Thomas contributed was not limited to mere theory, profound and brilliant as it was. No, he saw catechesis as essentially pastoral and therefore practical. And so we have our second great moment in the history of the transmission of the Faith to us. This moment occurred when St. Thomas turned to devote the last best years of his life, not to theology (that had become "straw" to him!) but to catechesis. He left his great *Summa Theologica* unfinished and turned instead to a *Compendium Theologiae* and several "little works": the famous *Opuscula*, in which he taught, as if he were in a CCD class at the local parish, the Apostles' Creed, the Ten Commandments, the Our Father, and—encompassing them first and last—the sacraments.

THE MODERN CHURCH

From our first moment in the ancient Church with St. Augustine, through our second moment in the medieval Church with St. Thomas, we now proceed to our third moment. In the midst of the great crisis of Reformation and Counter-Reformation, which is generally recognized as marking the beginning of the modern Church, in the year 1566 occurred what is surely the greatest catechetical moment in the history of the Church to date: the publication of the Roman Catechism. The first official catechism for the universal Church, this little book deserves even more attention than what it has already received, for it is unquestionably, without precedent and without peer, the greatest single written witness and instrument of the Church's authentic catechesis—which makes it therefore the greatest single instance of the Church's Ordinary and Universal Magisterium.

Much indeed can be said about the Roman Catechism: but for our present purpose this brief resume must suffice. The classic catechesis finds in the Roman Catechism its perfect expression: in content, in structure, in spirit. The content is, as we have said earlier, "the Faith, the whole Faith, and nothing but the Faith." The structure is the fixed yet dynamic flow from Faith called hope and charity, articulated in the classic formulas of Creed, Commandments, and Prayer, and bound together as a kind of trinity in the living reality of the sacraments.

As for spirit, what this means concretely in real life will be better seen after we have finished our overview of the transmission of the Faith to our own times, by looking now at the fourth and final moment in our history of catechesis.

This final moment is occurring right now, marking as it does the end of the *modern Church* and the mysterious beginning of a *post-modern Church*—and coinciding (significantly enough) with the closing years of the second millennium and our entrance into the third where we find ourselves today. Corresponding to the position of the Roman Catechism in our third moment is that of the new Universal Catechism of the Catholic Church in our fourth moment. In October 1992 Pope St. John Paul II authorized its publication, with revisions to conform with the original Latin text published as a second edition in 1997.

Two observations can be made about the new Catechism. First, it will not—because it cannot—*supplant* the Roman Catechism, in the sense of relegating it to the status of a museum piece. Rather, it *supplements* the Roman Catechism, in the sense of adapting it to the exigencies of a new age in the history of the world and of the Church. The Roman Catechism will always remain what it is: a timeless statement of the classic—i.e., the timeless—catechesis.

Second, the new Universal Catechism can be—because it must be—judged in the light of three current documents of the Church's Ordinary Magisterium, namely Paul VI's *Profession of Faith* (commonly called "The Credo of the People of God") in 1968, the Holy See's *General Catechetical Directory* in 1971, and John Paul II's *Apostolic Exhortation Catechesi Tradendae* in 1979. These three documents give us, respectively, the content, the structure, and the spirit of the classic catechesis—that catechesis which from the beginning, through St. Augustine, through St. Thomas Aquinas, through the Roman Catechism, has transmitted to us the Faith.

Our profession of Faith that comes to us from the Apostles teaches us what we must do to become holy on our journey to eternal life. Through learning what the Church teaches, whether with formal study or individually, we can see how proper catechesis leads us to *know what the Church teaches*—and has always taught since the Apostles—so that we can develop and practice a Rule of Life that forms and guides us.

Understanding what the Church teaches about our Faith links us to the virtue of hope which in turn links to love, which is indeed the most important, in the sense that without it, all the previous links are literally worthless as far as our eternal destiny is concerned. Faith and hope are to charity what the booster rockets are to the payload: in the orbit of eternity only charity remains (1 Cor 13:1–3). Since that is so, it is most important that we understand correctly just how our formation in *charity*, as distinct from hope and faith, fits into the classic catechesis that we must know in order to understand the teachings of the Church ourselves and pass this knowledge on to others.

What may occasion a misunderstanding here is that very alignment of the three virtues with the three formulas of the ancient catechumenate, the articulation of which (as we have seen) may be considered the formal beginning of the classic catechesis itself. The Creed teaches us faith, the Our Father teaches us hope, the Commandments teach us love. This alignment is certainly true—as far as it goes. Love without the Commandments is even more a chimera than faith without the Creed or hope without prayer.

But leaving it at that is itself a chimera for all three, and especially for love. For the Commandments *as such* are at best the Old Law, and at worst the law of mere *nature*. What we are dealing with are Christians, who heed—and who have a claim to—more than what the Commandments *of themselves* can give. That need and that claim are based on their being Christian, i.e., their being baptized and now being essentially and intrinsically in the *sacramental* order.

Thus, what really teaches love, in the sense of *living* love and not merely knowing about it, is the *sacraments*.

The same holds true, of course, with both faith and hope as well. We may know the faith from the Creed, but we *live* the faith from the sacraments. We may know hope from the Our Father, but we *live* our hope from the sacraments. And why is this so? Because only in the sacraments do we have the "real presence" in us—individually and in community—of Our Lord Jesus Christ. We have the real presence of His action in all seven sacraments, and making that action real, the real presence of His Person in the Blessed Sacrament of the Eucharist.

Throughout this discussion we have seen the absolute importance of the word: the word at once human and divine, spoken and unspoken, written and unwritten. Our life depends on the word, yes: for the fulfillment as for the beginning of our life, the word is necessary. But this word is the *Word-made-flesh*. Our Liturgy of the Word at Mass leads to and is fulfilled only in the Liturgy of the Eucharist, the source and summation of the Christian life (*Lumen gentium*, no. 11).

Let our final word on our journey to live within the Sacred Heart of Jesus be this: faith, hope, and charity as they are found in the Creed, prayer, and the Commandments are essentially Christocentric. They have their beginning and their end and everything in between in the Person of Our Lord Jesus Christ. And Our Lord Jesus Christ is for us, here and now, the Holy Eucharist. Only in the Eucharist—as source and as transmission and as destination—can we fulfill our vocation to be with God forever in Heaven.

REFLECTIONS FROM THE SAINTS

"Act as if everything depended on you. Trust as if everything depended on God."—ST. IGNATIUS OF LOYOLA

"I plead with you—never, ever give up on hope; never doubt, never tire, and never become discouraged. Be not afraid."—POPE ST. JOHN PAUL II

"Live in faith and hope, though it be in darkness, for in this darkness God protects the soul."—ST. JOHN OF THE CROSS

"Lord, grant that I might not so much seek to be loved as to love."—ST. FRANCIS OF ASSISI

"Love, indeed, is the source of all good things. It is an impregnable defense, and the way that leads to Heaven."—ST. FULGENTIUS OF RUSPE

"Love Him totally Who gave Himself totally for your love."—ST. CLARE OF ASSISI

"All holiness and perfection of soul lies in our love for Jesus Christ our God, Who is our Redeemer and our supreme good."—ST. ALPHONSUS LIGUORI

C H A P T E R T W O

WHAT IS THE HOLY EUCHARIST? A BRIEF CATECHESIS

"I am the living Bread that has come down from Heaven. If anyone eats of this Bread he will live forever. And this Bread that I will give is My flesh for the life of the world" (Jn 6:51).

JUST AS OUR LORD JESUS CHRIST, SON OF God, Second Person of the Blessed Trinity, true God and true Man, is the sum and center of our life, so the truth concerning Him—the *Lumen Christi*—is the sum and center of this chapter in our journey to live within the Sacred Heart of Jesus. Here is presented yet more specifically and concretely the essential content of the Christian catechesis; what is has always been in the Catholic Church and what it must always be, if we are indeed to know Christ and to live His life *on His terms*. For the truth and life that is Christ is for us here and now, by His own institution and command, nothing other than the most Holy Eucharist.

This centrality and totality of the Holy Eucharist in our life as Christians is most beautifully expressed in the paragraph introducing the chapter entitled "The Most Sacred Mystery of the Eucharist" in the Second Vatican Council's Constitution on the Liturgy:

> At the Last Supper, on the night He was betrayed, our Savior instituted the Eucharistic Sacrifice of His Body and Blood. He did this in order to perpetuate the sacrifice of the Cross throughout the centuries until He should come again, and so to entrust to His beloved spouse, the Church, a memorial

> of his death and resurrection: a sacrament of love, a sign of unity, a bond of charity, a paschal banquet in which Christ is consumed, the mind is filled with grace, and a pledge of future glory is given to us. (*Sacrosanctum Concilium*, no. 47)

More succinctly and yet more comprehensively, this same doctrine of the Vatican Council is expressed in one sentence of its Constitution on the Church: The Holy Eucharist is the fount and apex of the whole Christian life (*Lumen gentium*, no. 11).

The Eucharistic doctrine of Vatican II was solemnly ratified and amplified by Pope St. Paul VI in an encyclical written toward the close of the Council and significantly entitled *Mysterium Fidei*. The Holy Father tells us there is really no other mystery of faith like that of the Eucharist, for "properly speaking . . . it *is* the Mystery of Faith" (no. 15). And he quotes his predecessor, Leo XIII: "In the Holy Eucharist alone are contained, in a remarkable richness and variety of miracles, *all* supernatural realities."

There is profound significance in the fact that the Holy Eucharist is not explicitly mentioned in either the Apostles' Creed or the Nicene Creed. It is not a "part" of the Creed because it is the *whole* Creed! It is the summation, by Our Lord's own words and actions, of all that He would have us believe. "Christ has died, Christ is risen, Christ will come again." In the one "Mystery of Faith" that is the Eucharist, we proclaim all our faith. For in it alone we remember Him as He wills to be remembered, we await Him as He wills to be awaited, we possess Him as He wills to be possessed.

No, just as this one rich and simple intuition of the faith had to become explicit in its parts, just as the white Light of Christ is prismed through the Church into our multi-colored articles of faith, so too we must be somewhat analytical. By proceeding from part to part, we first learned our faith and grew deep within it; by this same process must we learn to teach it to others. Thus, there are five parts to our discourse on how we can learn what we need to know about the Holy Eucharist so that we will be able to teach it to others—our family members, catechumens, friends interested in knowing why we believe that Jesus Christ is fully present in the Holy Eucharist, and most importantly, how we ourselves can come to have an overwhelming desire and love for the Holy Eucharist.

First, we will consider what Christ intended to do, and what He does, in the Holy Eucharist. Second, what is and must be the basis of this action of Christ. Third, what is the basis of the Church's response to this? Fourth, what has been and is the response itself on the part of so many—too many—to the Holy Eucharist? And finally, what is or should be our response to it as we journey toward life in the Sacred Heart of Jesus through our total love of the Holy Eucharist.

WHAT CHRIST INTENDED TO DO

What Our Lord Jesus Christ intended to do is revealed in His words as recorded in the unforgettable sixth chapter of St. John's Gospel. "I am the living Bread that has come down from Heaven. If anyone eats of this Bread, he will live forever. And this Bread that I will give is My flesh, for the life of the world" (Jn 6:51). His flesh, His very Body—to be eaten. What an image!

If this were but an image, a figure of speech, it would be as inappropriate as it was abhorrent—especially to anyone raised in the law of Moses which sternly proscribed the eating of flesh with blood (Lev 17:11). For "to eat the flesh" of someone is a Biblical image of mortal enmity (as, for instance in the second verse of the Twenty-Sixth Psalm). It would be anything but the image of unity and love that Christ would have evidently intended.

No, His words are to be taken as literally true. Indeed, He was so understood by those who heard Him, for they asked: "How can this man give us his flesh to eat?" (Jn 6:53). And because of this "hard saying," many of them could no longer follow Him (Jn 6:61, 67).

On these words, then, these words that promised the gift of His living Body as their food, depended the faith and following of the Twelve. They did believe and they did follow Him; and one year later, in Jerusalem, there to celebrate the Paschal feast, Jesus fulfilled by word and action what He had promised.

He took bread and broke it and gave it to them, saying, "Take this and eat of it, for this is My Body that will be given up for you." And likewise the chalice he gave to them, saying, "Take this and drink from it, for this is the chalice of My Blood that will be shed for you. Do this in remembrance of Me" (Mt 26:26–28; Mk 14:22–24; Lk 22:19–20; 1 Cor 11:23–25).

Thus were His actions and words to become our own, as we recall His death by receiving into our bodies His living Body, the true and living Passover of the Lord.

The Holy Catholic Church, through the priesthood He instituted that same night, has fulfilled His promise by renewing what He did. Under the appearances of bread and wine, His living Body and Blood renew the Paschal Mystery: He "passes over" in His Body to His Father, while at the same time He abides in His Body with us. These two motions—His Sacrifice to His Father, and His Communion with us—are but one motion, the one total motion of His Heart. He cannot go to His Father without us, for we are the completion of His Body. And He cannot abide with us without His Father, for in their mutual Holy Spirit Son and Father are one.

So, in answer to our first question: what happens in the holy Eucharist? What does Christ do in it? We say with the Church that Christ does *all* in it. Here and now and until the end of time He dies upon His Cross, for by His institution and command we recall that death from the past and make it present. Here and now he is risen and is still with us, for again by his institution and command we bring down from Heaven the Lord of Glory Who sits at the right hand of His Father. And here and now He judges us, for again by His institution and command we anticipate the end of time and our own resurrection. His death out of the past and our death out of the future now coincide, and what Christ Jesus does in His Eucharist is give us his Life!

This indeed is what He does. But now, what is the basis, the ground, for this action of His? Why is He thus able to act? What is the ultimate reality behind His action, so fundamental and necessary that without it the action itself loses its reality and becomes merely symbolic?

To ask the question is almost to answer it. Action is not subsistent in itself; it follows upon *being*. Christ acts in the Eucharist because He *is* in the Eucharist. This *being* of Christ under the appearance of bread, the Eucharistic existence of the Lord, is itself the sign—the efficacious sign—of what He does here: His Sacrifice and His Communion. This Sacrifice and this Communion *are* Christ, because He is totally present in His action. And He is so, because He says He is so. "This is My Body; this is My Blood."

The simplicity, the starkness of these words struck the Apostles to their heart on that night of betrayal. They could not see the effect of His words, but His words were enough. "Lord, to whom shall we go? You have the words of everlasting life" (Jn 6:69).

It was the everlasting livingness of these words that made it impossible for the Apostles not to do what He had done and at His command. "The bread that we break, is it not the communion of the Body of Christ?" (1 Cor 10:16). The reality of the Paschal Mystery—the reality of both the Communion and the Sacrifice—is grounded in the reality of the Body: the Real Presence here and now of the one living Body of the Lord.

THE CHURCH'S RESPONSE

If the Real Presence is therefore the basis of Christ's Eucharistic action, what is the basis of the Church's response to the Real Presence? It is, and can be, only one thing: recognition of *mystery*. Now, "mystery" in its most radical and ancient sense is not so much a proposition, an object of knowledge, that is hidden from us, as it is rather a thing, an object of cult, that is revealed to us. *Mysterium* and *sacramentum* are Latin synonyms for the same wondrous thing: a sacred sign that reveals the holiness, the majesty, the saving power of a god. So wondrous indeed is the sign that "mystery" eventually takes on its more immediate and modern sense—the hidden, the secret, the coded truth. But always the objective precedes the subjective, the thing revealed precedes the truth believed, the mystery precedes the faith.

That there has in fact been faith on the part of the Church in this mystery of the Real Presence — that this Mystery has always been called in even the most ancient liturgies the "Mystery of Faith" — is itself a fact that no one does or can deny. From the very beginning the Church has discerned in the breaking of bread the Body of her Lord only by faith. And she has counted herself blessed for so believing. "Blessed are they who have not seen but have believed" (Jn 20:29). Keeping His words and pondering them in her heart (Lk 2:19), the Holy Church, our mother, moves through this world toward the *vision* that awaits and beckons her.

For if by faith we see only as through a glass darkly (1 Cor 13:12), yet it *is* seeing! It is the beginning, tiny but sure, of that Blessed Vision that will last forever.

The Church has made some progress since that first night when Our Lord Himself remarked how little His Apostles then knew or even could bear (Jn 16: 12–13). With the sure instinct of that Holy Spirit that He promised her, the Church *sees* that the Holy Eucharist is less an object of study than an object of prayer. Speculation is often presumptuous and vain, but contemplation is never such. And so the Bride of Christ has adorned His Body, as by her contemplation of this Mystery of Faith she weaves the traditions of centuries into a seamless robe for Him — the robe of adoration and thanksgiving, of contrition and imploring prayer. Just as her faith has fashioned her prayer, so in turn her prayer has formulated her faith.

Out of the prayerful celebration of this Mystery of the Eucharist came the apology of Justin Martyr and the ecclesiology of Ignatius of Antioch. Out of the prayer of the Martyrs came the treatises of the Fathers — from Polycarp to Cyril, from Cyprian to Augustine. The Patristic theology was the Apostolic faith enriched by time and the gifts of the Holy Spirit gained in prayer.

The formulation of the Faith continued in the multifaceted milieu of a Christian culture — missionary and monastic, institutional and charismatic, theological and devotional — until certain formulas were reached and ratified as stating what it was that all along the Church believed. A term was finally found to express our faith in the Real Presence, as were "consubstantial" for our faith in the Holy Trinity or "one person" and "two natures" for our faith in the Incarnation. That term was "transubstantiation."

As canonized by the Magisterium in the Fourth Council of the Lateran in 1215, "transubstantiation" denotes the change of the total substance of the bread into the total substance of the Body of Christ, and of the total substance of the wine into the total substance of the Blood of Christ, with the result that nothing of the bread and wine remains but only their appearance (Denzinger, no. 802).

Lest there be any doubt, such as was raised by the Protestants some centuries later, that this formula is not apt or adequate for this Mystery, the Council of Trent in its thirteenth session solemnly confirmed it. What it confirmed was not an "explanation" of a mystery—for mysteries are never "explained"—but rather an expression of a fact: the fact of the Eucharistic presence of Christ as being a true, real, and substantial presence (Denzinger, nos. 1636, 1651).

If it be contended that the formula, transubstantiation, sounds "philosophical," conditioned by an outmoded Scholasticism, let it be stated that indeed so it *sounds*. But what is important here is not the sound but the *sense*. We may well say that not in spite of but precisely because of this discrepancy in sound and appearance, transubstantiation is a most apt and adequate formula for this Mystery—this Mystery that the Church has learned not by her study but by her prayer.

So the Schoolmen joined the Fathers in their common contribution to the enrichment of our vision in our faith, gained by time and the gifts of the Holy Spirit in prayer. It is therefore no coincidence at all that the greatest of the Schoolmen, the incomparable St. Thomas Aquinas, composed the hymns for the newly instituted liturgical feast of Corpus Christi. Thus, both philosophy and poetry assumed their rightful roles as acolytes in the procession of prayer ordered by the Holy Church to honor her Mystery of Faith!

So great was the work of the Council of Trent, confirming Lateran IV and fixing by formulation the faith of the Church in the Sacraments of Christ, that the Church's Magisterium in our modern times has had but to remind us of that faith, to renew us in our prayer and practice of the Sacraments, and to warn us of the dangers that come from their misuse and neglect. This pastoral role of the modern Church is most evident in the work of the Second Vatican Council and of our recent popes, for they simply take the Tridentine formulations, tell us that this is the faith of the Church, and urge us to live that faith.

This brings us to the two concluding parts of our discourse: the response to the Holy Eucharist on the part of those who do not believe and on the part of those who do.

THOSE WHO DO NOT BELIEVE

By "those who do not believe," we mean those who do not believe *as the Church believes*. For the only faith that is really faith, as proportioned to the Mystery, is the faith of the Church. We as individuals only share in that faith of the total Body, incorporated into it by baptism and ratifying that incorporation by confirmation and obedience.

Therefore, we include among the unbelievers those who may say they believe—and indeed may mean what they say—but who do not accept the fact of the Real Presence as expressed by the formula, transubstantiation. They may consider that term irrelevant or even erroneous; they may substitute some other formula such as "transignification" or "transfinalization" or whatever. They may perhaps adopt no formula at all.

What these people actually believe concerning the Eucharist is often very difficult, if not impossible to say; but what they do *not* believe is quite simple to say. They do not believe in the "total substance" of the Body of Christ in the Holy Eucharist, with no other "substance" there—only the appearance of bread. They do not believe in the total *being* of Christ's Body sustaining and "realizing" His actions of sacrifice and communion. And because they do not believe this, they cannot do what the Church does: adore Christ's Bodily Being in the

Eucharist, seeing the Tabernacle on her altar as Heaven itself.

If it is relatively simple to say *what* they do not believe, it is almost as simple to say *why* they do not. At no great risk of oversimplification, I think the grounds of this disbelief are basically two. And as is usually the case in these matters, they seem to be at opposite extremes.

On the one hand there are those for whom the authentic Catholic doctrine of the Real Presence is a scandal, because it embodies a Body—and bodies, even Christ's Body, are somehow vile! This is the primeval heresy of the Gnostics, for whom Christianity is the pure religion of the spirit and must be lived—can be lived—only by the repudiation of the body. What is really scandalous to them is, of course, the Incarnation itself. And the Holy Eucharist, which is the ultimate epiphany of the Incarnate God, is the ultimate scandal.

On the other hand, there are those for whom the authentic Catholic doctrine of the Holy Eucharist is also a scandal, not because a Body is there, but because the *wrong* Body is there! If the Church has supposed over all these centuries that the Body spoken of by Christ is the same Body that was born of the Virgin Mary and suffered under Pontius Pilate, then the Church is simply mistaken. For, now we are told, *that* Body is dead! The only "Body" Christ has now—and has ever had since His death—is *ourselves*!

The bodily Resurrection of Him Who was crucified is, now we are told, a myth—emptier of historical fact than the so-called "empty tomb." We, the disciples who believe in His "Spirit"—we are now told—*we* are His Body and He lives now in us.

We feed on the memory of the historical Jesus, and we aspire in some evolutionary process toward the cosmic Christ. In such a scheme of things there is still room for some kind of "Lord's Supper," some symbolic prop for a community's memory and a community's aspiration.

But there is no room for a tabernacle! The presence of an altar and of a living Body on that altar, Who is not "becoming" anything, but is already totally existent, totally human and totally divine—*that* kind of Body is more than an embarrassment. It is a positive scandal!

And so the scandal is compounded. Despite seeming contrariety between two extremes, the Dualists and the Positivists—the "Church of the Spirit" and the "Church of the People"—agree in their scandalized denial of the Church's faith in the Real Presence of the one Christ Jesus: God enfleshed by the reality of body, and ensigned by the appearance of bread.

WHAT ABOUT WE WHO DO BELIEVE?

So much for those who do not believe, who indeed are scandalized by this Mystery of Faith. What are we now, and finally, to say about ourselves? We do believe as the Church believes, and we therefore share in her blessings: blessed for not seeing and yet believing in Christ (Jn 20:29); blessed for not being scandalized in Him (Mt 11:6).

Our Lord anticipated this scandal. He knew that He had come for the fall as well as for the resurrection of many in Israel, that He was a Sign of Contradiction (Lk 2:34). His Eucharist was a calculated risk: risking the neglect and positive desecration touching His Person because of it, risking the contention and disunity that would arise among Christians because of it, risking the very perversion of His chosen sign of peace and unity and love. Perhaps, in view of all this, we should say it was *not* calculated, that He Himself rather than Judas was His real betrayer—giving Himself into the hands of sinners out of an uncalculating, unfathomable love.

We must not, then, be scandalized, nor in our turn give scandal, especially to the little ones for whom Christ reserves a special providence of angels (Mt 18:6, 10). We must respond to the love of Christ by first of all *believing* in it.

This Holy Eucharist *is* His sign—and, being His, it *is* efficacious—of the unity and peace and charity that is His with his Father in Their Holy Spirit. That peace and unity and charity, that grace and glory, are realized here and now in this Agape to which we are bid, to feast on the first fruits of Paradise. That we do not taste and see as we ought is due not to Him but to ourselves. What, then, are we to do?

We are to do what the Church has always done in the

presence of the Mystery of Faith: we are to *pray*! If knowledge precedes and service follows, as indeed they should, prayer is the center, the living center of the Christian life. And that center, as we have seen is where the Holy Eucharist is.

Specifically and concretely, I recommend two kinds of prayer, enclosing as it were the centrality and totality of the Eucharistic Body of Christ.

First, the prayer of *purification*, by which we come to our Mass and Holy Communion with real repentance, seeing as we do the abyss that separates this awesome Mystery from our sinfulness and misery and that of the world. This repentance was enjoined on us from the beginning. "Let a man prove himself," St. Paul warns, "and so let him eat of this bread"; for otherwise he eats judgment to himself, not discerning the Body of the Lord (1 Cor 11:28–29).

By her growing awareness of the Mystery, the Church has made more specific the minimal meaning of this repentance: we dare not, under pain of sacrilege, approach this Sacrament of the Living while in the state of mortal sin. Sacramental confession is necessary in such instances, and most salutary in all instances, as the most fitting preparation for the Holy Eucharist.

As the prayer of purification precedes the Eucharistic action, so the second kind of prayer I recommend follows it. For want of a better word, I call it the prayer of *celebration*. Following the action of Christ in the Mass itself, with the official liturgical celebration by the priest and with the people participating in their proper role, there remains our informal and unofficial "celebration"—our bearing His action, His "good news" back into the world, while still somehow remaining, as He remains in His house on earth, His tabernacle-tent sheltering Him and us on our journey home.

Eucharistic devotion—our prayer of celebration—is integral to our living the Mystery of Faith. Whether this devotion is public—with Exposition and Benediction, or with prayer in common—or whether it be private, alone before the altar in silence—this prayer celebrates indeed not only the action but the *being* of the Lord!

If, in conclusion, this reality of the Mystery of Faith is not yet as real in us as it is in Him, then we know exactly what to do! We turn in prayer, at once repentant and rejoicing, to Him—Jesus Christ, yesterday, today, and the same forever—at once hidden and revealed in His Mystery, now hidden and revealed in our hearts.

REFLECTIONS FROM THE SAINTS

"If you ate only one meal a week, would you survive? It is the same for your soul. Nourish it with the Blessed Sacrament." —ST. ANDRÉ BESSETTE

"When the bee has gathered the dew of Heaven and the earth's sweetest nectar from the flowers, it turns it into honey, then hastens to its hive. In the same way, the priest, having taken from the altar the Son of God (who is as the dew from Heaven, and true son of Mary, flower of our humanity), gives Him to you as delicious food." —ST. FRANCIS DE SALES

"The more Eucharist we receive, the more we will become like Jesus, so that on this earth we will have a foretaste of Heaven." —ST. CARLO ACUTIS

"One of the most admirable effects of Holy Communion is to preserve the soul from sin, and to help those who fall through weakness to rise again. It is much more profitable, then, to approach this divine Sacrament with love, respect, and confidence, than to remain away through an excess of fear and scrupulosity." —ST. IGNATIUS OF LOYOLA

"If it is 'daily bread,' why do you take it once a year? Take daily what is to profit you daily. Live in such a way that you may deserve to receive it daily. He who does not deserve to receive it daily, does not deserve to receive it once a year." —ST. AMBROSE OF MILAN

"Upon receiving Holy Communion, the Adorable Blood of Jesus Christ really flows in our veins, and His Flesh is really blended with ours." —ST. JOHN VIANNEY

"Christ is both the priest, offering Himself, and Himself the Victim. He willed that the sacramental sign of this should be the daily sacrifice of the Church, who, since the Church is His body and He the Head, learns to offer herself through Him." —ST. AUGUSTINE

CHAPTER THREE

DISCERNING THE BODY OF THE LORD: WHO MAY RECEIVE THE EUCHARIST?

"I tell you most solemnly, if you do not eat the flesh of the Son of Man and drink His blood, you will not have life in you. Anyone who does eat my flesh and drink my blood has eternal life and I shall raise him up on the last day" (Jn 6:53–54).

IN THESE TROUBLED TIMES, WE CAN SURELY do no better than to reflect on the central mystery of our faith: the most Blessed Sacrament. It is central because it is simply *the* Mystery of Faith. To illumine this mystery is the ultimate total purpose of all genuine Catholic catechetical instruction. Or rather, we should say more accurately, it is we who are illumined by this mystery.

This is an occasion to be illumined by the Church, both from the sources of her faith and from the decisions of her prudence, on what is surely the most current and urgent pastoral question concerning the Blessed Sacrament, namely, who may receive the Holy Eucharist?

The present discussion can be conveniently divided into three parts. First, let us reflect upon this use of the sacrament, or—as the ancients would say—on its "economy." Let us see how this "economy" is best summarized by that one rich and resonant word—itself most classical—the word "communion." Secondly, let us see how in the course of her history, and particularly in the twentieth century, the Church has developed this "economy," i.e., how both the doctrine and the discipline of "communion" have grown.

Thirdly and finally, let us reflect once more, this time on the "theology" of this development, seeing how it is best summarized by that one small phrase from St. Paul's First Letter to the Corinthians, at once so awesome and so consoling: "discerning the Body of the Lord" (1 Cor 11:29).

THE "ECONOMY" OF THE HOLY EUCHARIST

Beginning now with the first part, "economy," we must remind ourselves that although these two things — economy and theology — are distinct, they are nevertheless inseparable, in the same way that the doctrinal and the disciplinary or pastoral are distinct but inseparable. This fact of distinction and inseparability is true of all the mysteries of our faith, even of such totally transcendent mysteries as that of the Blessed Trinity. Its economy, as revealed in Scripture, led to its theology, as formulated in the Creed.

It is all the more true of the Mystery of Faith, this mystery that is in our very midst, which is the Holy Eucharist. Of all the heavenly things revealed and given to us by God, here surely is the Thing that by its very nature of *sign* is meant to be *used*.

How often have we heard the current remark: "Christ in the Eucharist is not meant to be in a golden box, but in *us*. He comes as food, and food is for eating." Yes, that is true. Although we must not overlook the latent danger of the negation ("He is *not* meant to be in the tabernacle"), we cannot on that account deny the truth of the affirmation: He *is* meant to be in us. Our Lord indeed instituted this mystery in order to be *present* to us. This means that He is there, in the total reality of His Person.

But it also and equally means that *we* are to be there too, in the total reality of our person. And the two of us — Christ and the Christian — become *one* by means of a Sign that effects what it signifies and signifies what it effects. And that Sign is food.

Christ comes, then, clearly *down* to us, yes—even as bread into our bodies. To take this literally is a "hard saying," to say the least (cf. Jn 6:60). But in the very face of that reaction, Christ's response was a repetition—and a clear command. "Take this, all of you, and eat" (Mt 26:26). And why? In order to have *life* in you: the real life, the only life that will never die.

And so, if Christ comes down to us to be eaten, it is only in order that we may go *up* to Him to live. For He will not be changed into us, as earthly food is changed. Rather, He—the food from Heaven—will change us into Himself.

In this imperative sentence of Christ, "Take and eat," which is every bit as unequivocally and scandalously clear as the declarative sentence that accompanies it, "This is my Body," we have the *use* of the Eucharist following its *being*. The bread is the efficacious Sign of His Body, and His Body is the efficacious Sign of eternal Life.

To become one with the divine Person of Jesus Christ by means of His sacred Humanity under the appearance of bread is what we mean when we say, "Holy Communion." "Holy Communion" is thus the finality of the Holy Eucharist.

Just as in the order of time it follows the consecration and completes the Sacrifice of the Mass, so in the order of nature it follows the Real Presence of Christ and completes its purpose, namely, to renew in us that same presence, which is for us a new nature; the divine nature itself. In the present life this communion with the divine nature is called "sanctifying grace." And in the life to come it is called "glory" or "beatitude" or simply Heaven.

If Holy Communion is literally the anticipation of Heaven, there is evidently nothing in this world that approaches even remotely its importance. It is the incomparable moment when Heaven is actually here and now in our exile, and we touch our homeland—and become "naturalized" to it. And this anticipation is given us, not merely to sustain us until we get there definitively in the life to come, but to enable us to get there at all. "Unless you eat the flesh of the Son of Man and drink His blood, you will not have life in you" (Jn 6:53).

This necessity is reflected in the urgency that Christ frequently manifested, even before that final Pasch which He so ardently desired. There are His parables of the great feast He had prepared (cf. Lk 14:16–24; Mt 22:1–10), and of His desire that His table be filled. Indeed, He would have his servants actually *compel* them to come in, gathering up the poor and maimed and blind and lame and whomever along the highways and hedges—"so that my house and my table may be filled" (Lk 14:23).

The holy Catholic Church, custodian and minister of the sacred mysteries, has heeded the words of her Lord, these words of His which are no less insistent in His invitation than in His institution. She has in fact made the simple and clear equation of "Holy Communion" with her entire life and being. "Communion" is the same word she uses interchangeably to designate this sacrament and to designate herself. The *sacra communio* is the *communio sanctorum*: the communion of the saints, the holy People of God. Do we not ourselves informally but really gauge the degree of our Catholic identity and participation by the degree of our being communicants of the Holy Eucharist?

This identification of the Church with and by the Holy Eucharist (and vice versa) on the level of "economy" is grounded, of course, in the theological truth of the ultimate *unicity* of the Body of Christ. The same one Body that was born of the Virgin Mary, that suffered, died, and was buried, that rose from the dead and is now seated at the right hand of God, is now also in the Eucharist, and in the Church.

Indeed, it *is* the Eucharist, and it *is* the Church—not in the same sense, obviously, but in a mutually complementary sense. The Real Presence of Christ's Body under the Eucharistic species is the cause of His presence in the members of the Church. This presence is, of course, the *communio*—at once Eucharistic and ecclesial—of which we speak. And this presence is what in turn ultimately explains, by virtue of the sacramental character of Orders, the Church's possession of and power over the Holy Eucharist.

But now, in keeping with our outline as stated, let us defer going into this theological reflection of Eucharistic-ecclesial communion until later. In this first part of our discussion we are considering only its economy; and we can now conclude this part by saying simply that the Church has indeed *used* this sacrament as Our Lord intended, and that in this use she has found the very principle and sign of her life by which she is identified with all that is within herself and distinguished from all that is outside herself. She and her Eucharistic Lord make indeed *one* "Communion."

A LOOK INTO HISTORY

This brings us to the second part of our discussion, namely, how in the course of time, and particularly in the past century, the Church has *developed* this economy of the Eucharist. This development has been practically identical with that overall development of the Church's consciousness of her unity and catholicity that is so characteristic of the twentieth century, i.e., of the two Councils of the Vatican, first beginning in 1869 with Vatican Council I and then in 1962 with Vatican Council II.

Through these two Councils, the Church has seen with ever greater clarity her role as the one Church, the one Sacrament of Salvation, for *all* mankind. She must eventually fill the Lord's table with guests: those dispersed children of the entire human race (cf. Jn 11:52), whose destiny is to be *her* children, at her table with the Lord.

It is a historical fact, and one going back to the first ages of her history, that the Church has progressively broadened the basis for participation in the great Banquet of her Eucharist. When the pristine practice of daily Communion slackened—because of factors totally other than her own official teaching—she prescribed as an absolute minimum, under the sanction of mortal sin, the so-called Easter Duty of annual Communion. This occurred at the Fourth Lateran Council in the early thirteenth century.

From there she proceeded, with an acceleration of articulation and authority, to a *maximum*: the urgent recommendation of daily Communion—as often, that is, as the Holy Mass itself would be offered and attended, and as often as we would pray as Our Lord taught us to pray—for our "daily bread." It is, moreover, interesting to note here how historically parallel were the developments in both the "theology" and the "economy" of the Eucharist.

The Tridentine Church which doctrinally defined the sacrament was the same Church which pastorally decreed the frequency of its use. And finally, it was at this same time generally that the Church confirmed the ancient practice of bringing the Holy Eucharist to the sick outside of Mass, and strengthened this practice by decreeing as a grave obligation the reception of the Eucharist as "Viaticum" by anyone in danger of death.

Thus, she also confirmed the practice of reserving the Eucharist, to be available at all times for adoration—no less than for reception—by her children. And thus, by the time of the First Vatican Council the Blessed Sacrament had become quite visibly what we might call both the "center" and the "circumference" of the Church, certainly coterminous with her life. What further developments could there yet be?

Coming to the twentieth century, we did see in fact a further development. Indeed, we saw two developments—one after the other—along this same line of broadened participation in the Eucharist, two developments of a yet more extensive and affective realization of the "Communion" of the Church.

The first was the epochal decision by Pope St. Pius X to equate the beginning of Eucharistic Communion with the beginning of the age of *discretion.* Henceforth, the "discerning the Body of the Lord"—meaning: the child's ability to distinguish between mere bread and the Body of Christ—would be coterminous with the receiving of that same Body.

And the second development was the similar decision by the Second Vatican Council to equate the range of Eucharistic Communion with the range of that same Eucharistic discretion. Henceforth, this same discerning of the Body of the Lord on the part of someone not yet totally in the visible Body of the Church would qualify that person (if at the same time he fulfilled certain definite conditions) to receive that same Body of Christ.

Thus, by two successive developments in the twentieth century, the inter-relationship of Eucharistic and ecclesial communion has reached a doctrinal and disciplinary precision which should make more evident both the unity and the catholicity of the Church—and her fulfillment of the intentions of Our Lord.

Assuming that by now—more than a century after the event—the first development, namely, that of St. Pius X's regarding the normalization of daily Communion and the extension of Communion to all persons in the Church who have attained the age of discretion, is sufficiently well known, we can proceed immediately to the second development, namely, that of the Second Vatican Council's regarding the extension of Communion to some persons who are not formally in the visible communion of the Church.

Over half a century has passed since this event; but judging from the prevalence of misunderstanding and misapplication that (for whatever reasons) it has occasioned, we must now look closely to what the Church has officially said on the matter in the Council itself.

The classic conciliar text occurs in the Decree on Ecumenism: *Unitatis redintegratio*. With delicacy and balance the Council Fathers state the principles, recognize the tensions, and anticipate the results. Let me quote the whole of Article 8 of this Decree, since the context of the statement is important here; and that context is one of prayer.

> [C]hange of heart and holiness of life, along with public and private prayer for the unity of Christians, should be regarded as the soul of the whole ecumenical movement, and merits the name "spiritual ecumenism."
>
> It is a recognized custom for Catholics to meet for frequent recourse to pray for the unity of the Church with which the Savior Himself on the eve of His death so

> fervently appealed to his Father: "That they may all be one" (Jn 17:20).
>
> In certain circumstances, such as in prayer services "for unity" and during ecumenical gatherings, it is allowable, indeed desirable, that Catholics should join in prayer with their separated brethren. Such prayers in common are certainly a very effective means of petitioning for the grace of unity, and they are a genuine expression of the ties which still bind Catholics to their separated brethren. "For where two or three are gathered together in my name, there am I in the midst of them" (Mt 18:20).
>
> Yet worship in common (*communicatio in sacris*) is not to be considered as a means to be used indiscriminately for the restoration of unity among Christians. There are two main principles upon which the practice of such common worship depends: first, that of the unity of the Church which ought to be expressed, and second, that of the sharing in the means of grace. The expression of unity very generally forbids common worship. Grace to be obtained sometimes commends it. The concrete course to be adopted, when all the circumstances of time, place, and persons have been duly considered, is left to the prudent decision of the local episcopal authority, unless the bishops' conference according to its own statutes, or the Holy See, has determined otherwise.

Faithful to the Gospel and the Tradition stemming from it, the Second Vatican Council thus faced the perennial paradox of Eucharistic Communion: the fact of its being at once the sign of an existing unity and the cause of a unity to be. Or, as the Council put it: this Communion as being on the one hand "the expression of the unity of the Church," and on the other hand "the sharing in the means of grace." It would resolve this paradox by leaving it to "the prudent decision" of the Church, on the universal and appropriate local levels.

Thus we have the authoritative decision of the Church on the conditions for Eucharistic Communion on the part of formal non-Catholics. They are five in number, and must be verified together: (1) the separated brother must be in a state of urgent need; (2) he must be in a position where access to his own minister is impossible; (3) he must spontaneously ask it of a Catholic priest; (4) he must profess the same faith in the sacrament that the Church professes; and (5) he must be rightly disposed.

THE PROVING OF OURSELVES

Now at last, we can proceed to the third and final part of our discussion: a reflection on the theology of this recent development in our Eucharistic-ecclesial communion in the Mystery of Faith. If, as we noted earlier, there was in fact a parallel development of discipline and dogma—of economy and theology—regarding the Holy Eucharist in the Tridentine Church, may we not dare to hope that a similar development is in God's providence awaiting us?

That which is common to both developments of the twentieth century is the *extension* of Eucharistic Communion to two groups of baptized persons: in the first development, under St. Pius X, to children in the Catholic Church, and in the second development, under Paul VI, to certain needy persons outside the Catholic Church.

But more important than this extension, which in itself is merely quantitative, is the *intention* which justifies and legitimates it, which in itself is qualitative. This intention can only be identified as *faith*. And that faith can best be designated by the Pauline phrase: "discerning the Body of the Lord."

Curiously enough, the phrase itself never occurs in any of the documents: neither the *Sacra Tridentina Synodus* of 1905 nor the *Quam singulari* of 1910, nor any of the conciliar and Pauline documents cited here. Nevertheless, the sense of the phrase is clearly evident in all of them. In *Quam singulari*, for example, we read that the norm which should determine a child's readiness for first Holy Communion is his ability "to distinguish the Bread of the Eucharist and ordinary material bread." Is this not exactly what St. Paul means by "discerning the Body of the Lord"?

Again, in the *In quibus rerum circumstantiis*, we read that the norm for a non-Catholic desiring to receive Holy Communion is "to manifest a faith in the Eucharist in conformity with that of the Church, i.e., in the Eucharist as Christ instituted it, and as the Catholic Church hands it on." Is this not again exactly what St. Paul means by "discerning the Body of the Lord?"

It is this *discernment*, therefore, this *active and articulated faith*, which is the principle, the all-important prelude to the use of this sacrament as willed by Christ and as administered by His Church. It is this discernment, this active and articulated faith, which fulfills Christ's words of invitation, because it first recognizes His words of institution. Here indeed is where we come in, in this: the Mystery of Faith!

Now it is true, of course, that this active and articulated faith is of itself insufficient for the worthy use of this sacrament. That is why we called it only the "prelude" to its use. What is further necessary is the *state of grace* and the *right intention*. (The necessity of these two conditions should be obvious: food can be eaten only by one who is already alive; the Eucharist is the Sacrament of the Living by very definition and the intention must be at least non-contradictory to the intrinsic "intention" of the divine life of grace within us.)

This necessity of grace and right intention is also clear from St. Paul himself in this same passage, since he tells us that we are to "prove" ourselves before partaking of this Bread, and that our "discerning" is itself both the purpose and the result of that "proving" (cf. 1 Cor 11:28).

But this very role of active and articulated faith—as the discernment of the Body, and therefore as the normal prelude to grace—is for that very reason all the more momentous. That is why, on the one hand, the Church has normally *not* given the Holy Eucharist to baptized infants, even though, strictly speaking, they are both able and worthy to receive it. On the other hand, that is why the Church *does* offer the possibility of receiving the Eucharist to those non-Catholics whose faith is that true faith which discerns the Body of Christ and so proves them that they may approach that Body and eventually—by means of that very grace—be received into It.

For the faith we speak of is the *true* faith, not something magical or automatic or any of the other caricatures made by those who have no faith. And so great is the Church's awareness of its value as an *active* reality—articulated, conscious, befitting the age of reason—that she is actually willing to forego some good for some of her children (i.e., including even those baptized beyond her visible unity).

That common good is the participation—responsible and effective—in the total faith of her body in the total reality of His Body, made one with her. By this faith of hers she invents nothing; she only *discovers*. She only finds what is already there—there before her, by His initiative and His institution, namely His Body, signed by the appearance of bread.

As long as this sign of His choosing is there, He is there—totally present. And this is so whether anyone else is present or not, whether anyone discerns Him or not, whether anyone proves himself or not.

Here is the "scandal," yes, of these developments in discipline, namely, their possible peril to doctrine, and their personal peril to our souls. A lavish "economy" *can* mean an impoverished "theology." An abundant access to grace *can* mean an abundant abuse of grace. "Compelling all" to enter the wedding feast *can* mean that some will be present without wedding garments on (cf. Mt 22:11–14). And incidentally, this possible scandal applies at least as much to the reforms of Pius X as to the reforms of Paul VI: a random check on "children's Masses" might prove disconcerting.

THE RISKS CHRIST TAKES

But this very possibility of scandal and this warning of judgment only prove the more how seriously Our Lord and His Church look for our discerning faith, and the "proving" of ourselves that flows from it.

Indeed, so great is this evaluation and expectation on His part, that Christ actually assumes an additional risk in His insistence on our having this discerning faith. Almost as in His earthly life when, we are told (Mk 6:5), He could work no miracles because of the people's unbelief, so here in His Mystery of Faith He does—in some even profounder sense—make

His Presence dependent on our presence, on our faith.

If He can *remain* under His sacramental sign without us, He yet cannot *come* under that sign without us. For this coming He has made Himself dependent on His Church, in the person of His priest. Thus the sacramental character of Orders — that mysterious counterpart of the Real Presence as the *res et sacramentum* of the Eucharist — comes once again to mind, as the very crux of the theology of the Eucharistic development of our time.

Suffice it to say that in our time we have come to see more clearly than ever before the "ecclesial truth" of the Eucharist and the "Eucharistic truth" of the Church: by His Eucharist Christ causes the Church to exist as His Body, and by His Church He causes the Eucharist to exist as His Body — both being, distinctly but inseparably, the one same Body of the Lord.

This one same Body of the Lord — born of Blessed Mary, crucified, risen, and seated with the Father — is thus both the source and the completion, the efficient and the final cause, of the *communio* that is our beatitude both here and hereafter. Hereafter: we shall be with Him, and in Him — the *totus Christus*, the *solus Sanctus*; we shall be with all the saints.

But even here and now, we are with Him, by our union in the Holy Eucharist and in the Church. For here in this world of our mortality, the *communio* is intrinsically and necessarily both Eucharistic and ecclesial: indeed, it cannot be the one without the other.

If it is true that charity must precede our reception of the Eucharist (in the same way that faith must precede our reception of Baptism), it is yet equally true that charity needs the Eucharist for its life (in the same way that faith needs Baptism).

And so, in summary, we can say that just as there cannot be truth without charity and charity without truth, or unity without catholicity and catholicity without unity, so without the Holy Eucharist there can be no Church and without the Church there can be no Holy Eucharist.

Further and finally, just as truth and charity are ultimately one—for both are Christ, so the Eucharist and the Church are one—for both, ultimately and ineffably, are Christ.

I would like to conclude this discussion on a brief hortatory note. We live in a perilous time—perilous for its scandal. But blessed are we if we are not scandalized (Mt 11:6). This very peril can be for us a privilege—yes, a privilege for the very need we now have to *prove* ourselves! Our faith—our discernment of Christ and His Church, of His Word and His sacrament—must be a *living faith*: conscious, responsible, effective, active, and articulated. Only thus can we be worthy of the Viaticum that in God's providence awaits us, when we enter fully and finally into our "naturalized" homeland, our *patria* in the communion of the saints.

This living faith means, first and last, that we truly heed the Lord Christ's call to ourselves and to all mankind: the call of His Heart to come into and to remain in His Communion. And this true heeding means that we discern His Body and prove ourselves—and help others to do likewise—so that the House and Table of His Communion may at last be filled.

REFLECTIONS FROM THE SAINTS

"He said: 'This is my Body'; therefore, the Eucharist is not the figure of His Body and Blood, as some have said, talking nonsense in their stupid minds, but it is in very truth the Blood and Body of Christ."—ST. MACARIUS THE GREAT

"How many of you say: I should like to see His face, His garments, His shoes. You do see Him, you touch Him, you eat Him. He gives Himself to you, not only that you may see Him, but also to be your food and nourishment.... When the Mass is being celebrated, the sanctuary is filled with countless angels, who adore the Divine Victim immolated on the altar."—ST. JOHN CHRYSOSTOM

"If we but paused for a moment to consider attentively what takes place in this Sacrament, I am sure that the thought of Christ's love for us would transform the coldness of our hearts into a fire of love and gratitude."—ST. ANGELA OF FOLIGNO

"Recognize in this bread what hung on the Cross, and in this chalice what flowed from His side—whatever was in many and varied ways announced beforehand in the sacrifices of the Old Testament pertains to this one sacrifice which is revealed in the New Testament.... He who is all-knowing knew of nothing more that He could give than the Eucharist. He who is all-powerful could not do any more than He does in the sacrament and He who is all loving had nothing more that He could give. The Eucharist is a Divine storehouse filled with every virtue."—ST. AUGUSTINE

"What wonderful majesty! What stupendous condescension! O sublime humility! That the Lord of the whole universe, God and the Son of God, should humble Himself like this under the form of a little bread, for our salvation."—ST. FRANCIS OF ASSISI

"Open our ears to the Sacred voice of the wounds of Thy Body and Heart. These wounds are so many mouths through which You call to our hearts unceasingly. *Redite, praevaricatores, ad cor*: Return, you transgressors, to the heart, which means to My Heart that is all yours, since I have given it all to you. Return to the Heart of your Father, which is so full of love and mercy, which will receive you and welcome you, heaping upon you all His blessings."—ST. JOHN EUDES

"Have a great love for Jesus in His Divine Sacrament of Love; that is the divine oasis of the desert. It is the heavenly manna of the traveler. It is the Holy Ark. It is the life and Paradise of love on earth.... Live on the Divine Eucharist like the Hebrews did on the manna. Your soul can be entirely dedicated to the Divine Eucharist and very holy in the midst of your work and contacts with the world."—ST. PETER JULIAN EYMARD

CHAPTER FOUR

THE EUCHARIST: FROM HOLY COMMUNION TO ADORATION

"The blessing cup that we bless is a communion with the blood of Christ, and the bread that we break is a communion with the body of Christ. The fact that there is only one loaf means that, though there are many of us, we form a single body because we all have a share in this one loaf" (*1 Cor 10:16–17*).

WHEN POPE JOHN PAUL II IN 1997 announced the Holy Year of the Great Jubilee for the year 2000, he said it must be intensely Eucharistic. To symbolize that intention, the Eucharistic Congress was held in Rome.

It might surprise you, as it did many, that the Holy See did not give that much attention to the Holy Eucharist in the three years leading up to the Holy Year. Yet we do need to pay great attention to the Blessed Sacrament. The Holy Eucharist, as the Holy Father pointed out, is the *source and summit* of the Christian life, as is stated in Vatican II's Constitution on the Church, *Lumen gentium,* no. 11.

But the Holy Father put it in a context where he spoke of the *liturgy* as being the source and summit of the Christian life. He took a little liberty, though, as that is not exactly the text that appears in the document itself. The question I would ask is: In *what sense* is the liturgy the source and summit of the Christian life?

I would like to offer some context for this seeming hiddenness of the Holy Eucharist. The Holy Father is following a very, very ancient precedent, because if you stop and think about it, especially if you focus on the magnificent sixth chapter of St. John's Gospel, you will notice that the Eucharist is not mentioned all that many times in the New Testament—apart from chapter six of St. John, and two parts of St. Paul's Letter to the Corinthians, and the three institution narratives of the three Synoptics, Matthew, Mark, and Luke. Apart from these texts, there are just a few texts in the Canon where there is some kind of allusion to the Holy Eucharist. Otherwise, there is simply silence.

So we can conclude that Our Lord Himself intended the Holy Eucharist to be a kind of hidden thing—a hidden reality. That should not surprise us because after all it is a sacrament. It is *the* sacrament. And sacraments, as we all know, are things that are hidden. Christ in the Holy Eucharist is the reality hiding behind a sign.

Thus, the Holy Eucharist seems to be what it is *not*. It seems to be bread, but it's not. It seems *not* to be what it is. It *is* the Body of Christ, but it doesn't seem to be. Therefore, this hiddenness is something that is almost characteristic of the Holy Eucharist, so much so that without it, it really would not be what Our Lord intended. He intended it for His own. He intended it for the family. It is only within the household of the Faith that we can discern the Body of the Lord.

There is another sign for those outside the family: you are close to the sacraments if you love one another. *Charity* is the great sign which is unmistakable to the whole world. It was said in the early days of the Church: "See how those Christians love one another." But to see Christ Himself under the appearance of this little white disc is something beyond the possibilities and capabilities of human nature. *No one* can see Christ present unless they have *faith*.

So Jesus in the Holy Eucharist is hidden *deliberately*. In the New Testament the instinct of the early Church was to hide the reality of the Faith, this Mystery of Faith. It is not just *a* mystery, but *the* Mystery of Faith — the Holy Eucharist — the *disciplina secreti* — the discipline of the secret.

Back in the early Church, even the catechumens were not told about the Holy Eucharist until they were baptized. We called that distinction in the old days the Mass of the Catechumens and the Mass of the Faithful. The catechumens were dismissed from the Holy Mass right after the recitation of the Creed, when they were quietly and gently ushered outside. They were not there for the liturgy of the Eucharist. Why? Because they were not ready for it. They were not baptized and were not yet in the family. They were not yet in the know — the *know* which is Faith.

We come now to something which should be a matter of great concern to us, and that is because of all the secretness which continued for almost the whole first millennium up until about the year 1000. There's nothing in Denzinger's *Enchiridion Symbolorum* (which is a compilation of all the chief decrees of Church Councils) on the Holy Eucharist for those first thousand years. It's just not there.

Of course, we can say there was nothing there because of faith. There was just no problem to discuss. The Holy Eucharist was simply there and the faithful expected it to be there. The Holy Eucharist was too close to the Christian body for early theologians and Church Fathers to have a need to look upon it as some kind of thing for critical examination.

We can say about the first millennium of the Church that the Holy Eucharist was really just taken for granted. That's a rather equivocal term though, to take something for granted. It usually means we don't appreciate it. It's just something there. Perhaps we take the Holy Eucharist for granted because it is so close to us — we can't live without it — and we associate it with the very act of living itself.

WE SEE THE REALITY

The Holy Eucharist was taken for granted in some benevolent sense in that first millennium. But by an act of providence — God's providence — He saw to it in a marvelous way that the Church was reminded that there was something that needed to be done on all levels, from the clergy to the hierarchy, regarding this mystery in their very midst by which they were living. By virtue they were living to be the Church, because of the Holy Eucharist. And now God was saying to them: You must no longer take it for granted; it is necessary to look at it more intently. So God arranged for a few heretics to arise—there's always a purpose for heretics, you know.

I think we can thank God for these heretics. Where would we be without the dissenters? It's a blessing in disguise. It teaches us to value what we have, and not take it totally for granted, especially to examine it and verify it with the help of grace.

So when the second millennium began, sure enough, God had some good heretics lined up to prepare the Church to remind the people in the family that they must no longer take for granted this blessed thing that is the heart of the Church and that gives us life, the Holy Eucharist.

In those early years of the Middle Ages, there was a growing consciousness that the Holy Eucharist was not just something within us but was *something out there*, something objective, still within the family, within the boundaries of the household of the Faith. It was something to be looked upon, to be gazed upon, to be seen. In the liturgy of the Mass, the priest, after pronouncing the words, "this is my Body, this is my Blood," raises the Holy Eucharist aloft for all to see it, the Body of the Lord and the Blood of the Lord.

That was not part of the original rubrics from the Last Supper and the catacombs of Rome. But it was done here now in the second millennium. Many people think it is part of the Consecration, but it's not. It's a little embellishment, as it were. It's a sign that we are now to look upon the Blessed Sacrament.

It is something that is meant to be seen. Through our senses, we see the reality, and we believe it. St. Thomas Aquinas has a great exposition of this profound truth, a truth which the Church has always called the Mystery of Faith, not just *a* Mystery of Faith, but it is *the* Mystery. Everything is contained in it.

And so in the second millennium, here is what the Church did by the providence of God and the Holy Spirit: the Church developed an explanation of what exactly this Blessed Sacrament is—the Truth to be told to everyone in the family. The Church has always known, so much so that She did nothing to define it. But the Church now said that the Holy Eucharist is Christ the Lord in His Paschal Mystery: Christ has died, Christ is risen, Christ will come again. It's all right there in the action of the Mass—the one same sacrifice of Our Lord renewed, not multiplied, but renewed through all time and space until He comes again in glory.

That is what Our Lord intended to do at the Last Supper and what He did do. The Church has been faithful to Our Lord's command to the Apostles to do this in His memory—we do it and will continue to do it. The Holy Spirit will see to that until the end of time.

The whole of the sacrifice is the *action* of Our Lord, the magnificent reality of His magnificent invention, the invention of His prayer and the invention of His love. We have now in our possession, in the hands of our priests, the very sacrifice of His, and His Holy Commission to us. The action of Christ going to His Father—that is what the sacrifice is. I consecrate Myself, he said at the Last Supper, sending Himself to His Father. And by the same action, giving Himself to us.

So this action of giving Himself to His Father and giving Himself to us in Holy Communion seem to be distinct in themselves. In a sense they are distinct. Holy Communion without Mass is not the same as Mass with Holy Communion, true enough, even though the priest has to be the link between the two for real unity. But the analogy is perfect because of the virtue of charity. According to St. Paul and St. John, charity is two distinct things: love God and love our neighbor. They are the same unified. But so too the Holy Eucharist is not two different sacraments; the sacrifice and Holy Communion are the same thing, only two different facets of the one reality.

And the one reality is the reality of *activity*, of something that Christ does—the Holy Eucharist—giving Himself to His Father and giving Himself to us. We, by virtue of receiving Him, do the same thing. There's no way we can fulfill the One Great Commandment unless the Holy Eucharist is involved.

The Church has said throughout the centuries that outside the Church there is no salvation. That is perfectly true. We can also say that outside the Holy Eucharist there is no salvation. If there is no sacrifice, there is no communion, which means there is no love outside the Eucharist, *except by desire.*

The purpose of the Holy Eucharist is clearly what Our Lord intended it to be and what the Church has taught from the very beginning. It is the *action*, which is perfectly comparable to His Passion, which was His suffering. But the thing which made the Passion salvific was the action of His Heart. It was not the action of those who took His life, from Judas on down. It was His action of giving Himself to His Father and giving Himself to us.

THE REAL PRESENCE

From here we come to the Truth, our focal point—*the Real Presence*, a concept which we can say only really began in the second millennium. It's kind of an "extra"—something added now in God's Providence in the course of time, to reinforce, to lock in, as it were, the reality of Our Lord's action—the Mass and Holy Communion and the consecrated Communion Hosts being kept in reserve in a Tabernacle.

Already the concept of the Real Presence being kept in reserve was existing. Do not think otherwise, please, that this was some kind of invention on the part of the Church in the year 1000 or thereabouts. The Blessed Sacrament was always reserved—the sacrament outside of the Mass and Holy Communion, which means therefore about 23 hours of each day.

Day and night, where is the Lord? He's in His Eucharist *reserved*. Reserved for what? He is reserved primarily for the sick, particularly for those who need Holy Viaticum. When people are dying in hospitals or in their homes, and are not able to come to Church, Our Lord goes to them through his ministers the priests. He also goes to the men and women in jails and prisons who cannot come to Mass in the Church. Thus, the Holy Eucharist consecrated in the Mass *has to be* reserved.

It has to be kept in a little safe place, the Tabernacle. Sure enough then, the Church began to focus on this as the continuing sacrifice of Our Lord in Holy Communion as though He would always be in a state of sacrifice. Every reserved Host began with the Mass and ends with a Communion. This in no way destroys or impairs the unity of the sacrament. It only makes it clearer to us now.

You can see now the magnificence and inventiveness of Our Lord's power and love to be with us *always* as He promised. But we must remember on our part that there is a certain antecedence—a priority we must consider: how can Our Lord *act* unless he is there? It's as simple as that. *Action follows being* (*Agere sequitur esse*), St. Thomas Aquinas said in *De Potentia Dei* (q. 3, art. 1). The *being* of Our Lord is something antecedent, presupposed by His action. He cannot perform His sacrifice, He cannot give Himself to His Father unless He is there. This is what proves the doctrine of the Real Presence in the Eucharist and therefore, in a real sense, comes first.

In terms of our thinking and in terms of a certain pedagogy, a certain catechesis, this was all formalized by St. Thomas in the *Summa Theologica*—what the Church teaches about the Real Presence. As St. Thomas explained:

> The reality of Christ's presence in the Holy Eucharist "belongs to Christ's love, out of which for our salvation He assumed a true body of our nature. And because it is the special feature of friendship to live together with friends... He promises us His bodily presence as a reward... yet meanwhile in our pilgrimage He does not deprive us of His bodily presence, but unites us with

Himself in this sacrament through the truth of His body and blood." (*Summa Theologica*, III, q. 77, art. 1)

With that being the case, now we can talk about what Our Lord is *doing* while He is there in the Tabernacle and being taken to the sick, the dying, and prisoners by the priest. The purpose of the Holy Eucharist is not simply for Our Lord to *be* here residing in the Tabernacle after every Mass. Rather, it is because He has something to *do* here. But He cannot do it unless He is here.

So He has every reason then, every justification, to be something "separate," apart now from the Mass and Holy Communion—a reason to be there in the Tabernacle. The term "Blessed Sacrament" seems to be that—to be present in the little box called the Tabernacle as the sacrament in reserve, the reality of Our Lord, the Christ, the whole Christ, and nothing but the Christ. Somewhere in the world He is now offering His sacrifice at a Mass and giving Himself in Holy Communion until the end of time.

We are creatures of time and space and so He must be present to us on our terms. Thus, it is logical for Him to be present with us, and psychologically as well, as we need to feel the Holy Eucharist by knowing Our Lord is a little closer to us always in the Tabernacle. The Lord is in Heaven, but where is Heaven in space? We don't know that. But the Blessed Sacrament in reserve puts Him down here on our level deliberately. With the multiplication of churches and chapels, He is going to be somewhere near us, not too many miles away, unless we live in Alaska or some other place where a church is a day's journey or more away.

He is really there, inside the Tabernacle. We can more correctly say: He is really *here*. And we feel this. We Catholics instinctively feel this if we have any faith at all.

Just as that is true regarding space and time, the time we have to look backward to is the time of the New Testament when Jesus was alive. The Protestants find Our Lord in the Gospels and they learn them by heart. We should do that too. But the instinct we feel for the Gospels is in the past,

2,000 years ago. The Gospels are the past of Our Lord and the Apocalypse is His future. *But where is He now?* He's in the Tabernacle, that's where He is.

So looking through the lens of time and space, it seems that there is a profound instinct on the part of those who hold the Catholic Faith that there is a realization in terms of the Holy Eucharist of His presence to us. And from that flows the realization of what He does in Holy Communion.

It is in no way to be minimized. It is something profoundly real in Catholic life for Our Lord to be enabled to come closer to us as it was meant to be. In one respect, the Holy Eucharist is a mighty good disguise of His humanity. St. Thomas the Apostle says this is true in his doubting, saying he saw a man but did not see God. Then he said "my Lord and my God" after he first saw a man.

But St. Thomas Aquinas then went on to say "we don't even see a man. What we see looks like bread. But our instinct of faith tells us that it is not only God but man." There's something profoundly human about the Eucharist therefore, is it not? There's something profoundly human in the sense that it's tangible, it's approachable, it's vulnerable, mighty vulnerable.

He is in fact human, but at the same time He is divine as well. And the instinct of faith tells us that the Blessed Sacrament, that little approachable vulnerable thing, is divine because it manifests a power, an intimacy that is beyond humanity. If there is any self-proving Divinity on this earth, it is the Holy Eucharist.

So we have every reason to cherish this which is blessed, the reality of the Real Presence prescinding from the action of the Eucharist, which is the Mass and Holy Communion.

Now the Church gets into the act and gives us a clear teaching on this matter with three important texts.

First, from the Thirteenth Session of the Council of Trent in 1551, we have a Decree Concerning the Most Holy Sacrament of the Eucharist, chapter five, "On the cult and veneration to be shown to this most Holy Sacrament," which states:

> Wherefore, there is no room left for doubt, that all the faithful of Christ may, according to the custom ever received in the Catholic Church, render in veneration the worship of latria, which is due to the true God, to this most Holy Sacrament. For not therefore is it the less to be adored on this account, that it was instituted by Christ, the Lord, in order to be received: for we believe that same God to be present therein, of whom the eternal Father, when introducing him into the world, said: "And let all the angels of God adore him"; whom the Magi "falling down, adored"; who, in fine, as the Scripture testifies, was adored by the Apostles in Galilee.
>
> The holy Synod declares, moreover, that very piously and religiously was this custom introduced into the Church, that this sublime and venerable sacrament be, with special veneration and solemnity, celebrated, every year, on a certain day, and that a festival; and that it be borne reverently and with honor in processions through the streets and public places. For it is most just that there be certain appointed holy days, whereupon all Christians may, with a special and unusual demonstration, testify that their minds are grateful and thankful to their common Lord and Redeemer for so ineffable and truly divine a benefit, whereby the victory and triumph of His death are represented, And so indeed did it behoove victorious truth to celebrate a triumph over falsehood and heresy, that thus her adversaries, at the sight of so much splendor, and in the midst of so great joy of the universal Church, may either pine away weakened and broken; or, touched with shame and confounded at length, repent.

The Council then established several canons on the Most Holy Sacrament of the Eucharist, with canon six reinforcing the decree cited above:

> If anyone saith, that, in the Holy Sacrament of the Eucharist, Christ, the only begotten Son of God, is not to be adored with the worship, even external of latria; and is, consequently, neither to be venerated with a special festive solemnity, nor to be solemnly borne about in processions, according to the laudable and universal rite and custom of holy Church; or, is not to be proposed

> publicly to the people to be adored, and that the adorers thereof are idolators; let him be anathema.

The Church is saying that the Blessed Sacrament outside the celebration of the Mass, outside of Holy Communion, is to be adored the same way we adore the Father, Son, and Holy Spirit. The adoration is to be external, not just in the Tabernacle but in a monstrance on display. The Council of Trent in great detail defined the Mass and defined the Real Presence. Christ is *here* and he is here as long as the Blessed Sacrament is *here*.

The second major teaching about the Blessed Sacrament occurred in 1968 when Pope Paul VI issued the very solemn profession of faith called the *Creed of the People of God*. He explained transubstantiation and what the mysterious change achieves:

> Every theological explanation which seeks some understanding of this mystery must, in order to be in accord with Catholic Faith, maintain that in the reality itself, independently of our mind, the bread and wine have ceased to exist after the Consecration, so that it is the adorable Body and Blood of the Lord Jesus that from then on are really before us under the sacramental species of bread and wine, as the Lord wills it, in order to give Himself to us as food and to associate us with the unity of His Mystical Body.
>
> The unique and indivisible existence of the Lord glorious in Heaven is not multiplied but is rendered present by the sacrament in the many places on earth where Mass is celebrated. And this existence remains present, after the sacrifice, in the Blessed Sacrament which is, in the Tabernacle, the living heart of each of our churches. And it is our very sweet duty to honor and adore in the Blessed Host which our eyes see, the Incarnate Word whom they cannot see, and who, without leaving Heaven, is made present before us.

Beautiful words! We are to adore the Lord outside of Mass and Holy Communion *just because He is here in our presence*.

The third statement can be found in the law of the universal Church, canons 937 and 942, which state that churches must be kept open to the faithful for several hours a day so that they can pray before the Blessed Sacrament. We see that it is Church law that people must have some access to the Blessed Sacrament. Why? Access is needed to help people deepen their faith in it and to remind them that Jesus is there. The Blessed Sacrament is not to be forgotten. It's not to be tucked away in a closet somewhere. It is to be kept safe, for sure, because it is the most precious thing in this world and it is vulnerable. But it's meant to be *seen and loved* by the faithful.

We have every reason to be assured that adoration of the Blessed Sacrament is not just an act of devotion on our part, but it's a matter of Church law to make the Blessed Sacrament visible to the people in a Tabernacle or monstrance. The Real Presence of the Holy Eucharist is an intimate part of the Faith. It safeguards the supreme truth of the Faith and the supreme history of the Faith, which is Our Lord's sacrifice and communion.

The Church has reinforced the importance of the Blessed Sacrament in several documents following Pope Paul's encyclical *Mysterium Fidei* of 1965. Pope John Paul II wrote many documents and encyclicals about the Blessed Sacrament, and Pope Benedict XVI, in his Apostolic Exhortation *Sacramentum Caritatis* in 2007, articulated and emphasized the centrality of the Holy Eucharist to the very identity of the Church in its three dimensions: belief, celebration, and living. So no one can say that Eucharistic adoration is not the mind of the Church. You don't bury the treasure, the Church tells us. You *use* it! You adore it because it is alive and something that helps us multiply and build up grace in our souls—the faith and hope and love that saves us.

Talking about the Real Presence is solidly in the mind and the teaching of the Church. But there is something further that must be said. Vatican II said it is the *sacrifice* that is the source and summit of the Christian life—the *sacrificium Eucharisticum*. The Church is very clear that there is a profound respect for certain grades or certain levels, as it were, in the mystery of the Eucharist, which Our Lord Himself devised and which the Church preserves.

The Church has placed restrictions in her Code of Canon Law on the three stages of the Holy Eucharist. The sanctions for the three should make that quite clear.

First, we are to be attentive at Mass. There's no obligation to receive Communion, but the Mass—we had better be there or otherwise we may be in Hell. The priority of the Mass is a serious sanction (1983 Code of Canon Law, canon 898).

Second, the Church does not require us to receive Holy Communion every time we attend Mass, but only once a year—the Easter duty (canon 920). The reception of Holy Communion is integral to the Mass but the Church in her wisdom has made this distinction in terms of sanctions.

Third, the Church says that there is no obligation at all for the faithful to participate in adoration of the Blessed Sacrament. In the strongly worded canon 937, the Church says the Blessed Sacrament must be made available to the faithful: "Unless there is a grave reason to the contrary, a church in which the Blessed Eucharist is reserved is to be open to the faithful for at least some hours every day, so that they can pray before the Blessed Sacrament." As far as sanctions go, there is no sin if we don't go to adoration, whether in an adoration chapel where the Blessed Sacrament is exposed or simply praying in front of the Tabernacle.

While we hear criticisms from some of our more modern fellow Catholics telling us that adoration is simply an "embroidery" and not something necessary, the Church has a very clear mind about what is essential to us in our faith—adoration of Our Lord in the Blessed Sacrament—and we should have the very same clear mind as well.

BEAUTIFUL GRACE POURED OUT ON US

Going back to what Vatican II said about the Real Presence in that oft-quoted text, no. 7 of *Sacrosanctum Concilium*, the document on the sacred liturgy, there are different ways in which Our Lord is really present in the sacred liturgy. The key word is *real*. There are four ways in which He is present:

First, He is present in the minister—the priest or bishop. The priest does not say, "This is Christ's body." He says, "This is my body." The priest is saying "I am now Christ—He is really present in me and He speaks through me" here at the altar.

The second Real Presence is in the sacred species of the Eucharist, the bread and the wine that with the words of Consecration become the Body and Blood of Christ.

Third, He is really present in all the sacramental actions of the priest at the altar. The priest is acting as Christ Himself.

And finally, He is really present simply because He said so, that where two or more are gathered in my name, there I am with you in your midst (Mt 18:20). He is present in the body of the faithful attending the Mass.

Thus, there are four Real Presences in the unity of the sacred liturgy.

But the Council goes on to say that Jesus Christ is *maximus praesens*—He is most present—in the Eucharistic species.

This distinction has been misunderstood by many of the faithful, often due to being misled by their pastors, mostly by omission and negligence. Christ has a maximum presence in the Holy Eucharist as compared with His other presences, in that with the other presences of Our Lord, He is not *uniquely* there. We say He is uniquely there in the Holy Eucharist because the Eucharist is *all* Christ and nothing but Christ.

Yes, He is there in the other sacraments but there is something else there. In baptism, for instance, there is water there, real water, an essential component or sign of the sacrament of baptism. Christ is really present in the water by virtue of the Holy Spirit. That is why we speak of it as a spiritual presence. If the Holy Spirit wasn't there, nothing would happen.

It's a Real Presence, but it's a spiritual presence. Our Lord is not totally there—He's not there in His Body. There are other things besides Him that are there—the water—and the same thing happens with all the other sacraments, like the oil in confirmation and the imposition of hands in holy orders. Thus, we can say that the Real Presence of Christ in the other sacraments is almost an *alluded* presence. It's a Real Presence, but it is not a Eucharistic Presence.

Our Lord is not just in the Eucharist. Our Lord *is* the Eucharist. There's nothing else there. The only "things" are appearances—*species* in Latin. In the appearances—not just the visual appearances but anything that touches the senses like weight and size—Our Lord is there, Body, Blood, Soul, and Divinity. In fact, the Soul and Divinity are there only because the Body is there.

So, when we believe in the Holy Eucharist and we speak of the Real Presence, an essential aspect would be the real absence of anything *but* Christ. There is a real absence of bread. It's just simply not there. It may look like bread, but it's not.

Again we see that the Eucharistic Presence is a maximum presence. Our Lord Himself cannot be more present anywhere than He is in the Eucharist, so much so that if He were not in the Eucharist, He would be nowhere on this earth.

The Real Presence, using the word that the Council of Trent invoked for it, is *substantial* presence. The Church uses three words to describe the Holy Eucharist: true, real, and substantial presence. This substantial presence is found only in the Eucharist, not in the sacraments, not in the words of Scripture, not in the minister, not in the faithful. While Jesus is really present in the words of Holy Scripture, his Real Presence there is not substantial. He is not there in His Body, but in the Eucharist He is there in His Body, the same body that was born of Mary, died on the Cross, and rose from the dead, the same body that is in Heaven. That is the Mystery of Faith.

A second point is equally important. Why is the Holy Eucharist the maximum presence of Our Lord? It is the maximum presence because it is the *cause* of the other presences. The other presences of Our Lord, in the Sacred Scriptures for instance, are a consequence of His Eucharistic presence. It is true, especially as it applies to the other sacraments. If He is not present in the Eucharist, then He is not present anywhere.

This takes us back to the basic question: What is the Holy Eucharist? It is Our Lord's sacrifice, His primary action, and out of that sacrifice, the sacrifice of the Cross, comes *all* grace and *all* salvation. There is nothing apart from the Cross and therefore, all the efficacy of baptism and the other sacraments — everything in the Church — flows *from* the Holy Eucharist, not from the sacrifice of the Cross 2,000 years ago, but from the Holy Eucharist *here and now*. It's the same sacrifice. That is why the Holy Eucharist is the source and summit of the Christian life. The source and summit, the beginning and the end and everything in between. It's all right there in that little, tiny, round package.

The Holy Eucharist then helps us to live our life in the Church, a life of sanctifying grace, that grace which is Christ — His Body and His Blood, broken, given, and poured out for us — a great sacrifice, a great eternal sacrifice there in Heaven before His Father and sacramentalized for us here on earth.

Everything, absolutely everything, comes from that and flows back to it, the source and summit of the Christian life.

THE NEED FOR EUCHARISTIC ADORATION

To paraphrase Pope John Paul II in his 1997 letter introducing the Holy Year of 2000, we must be intensely Eucharistic, totally focused on the Holy Eucharist in our lives and not allowing anything to distract us from it, nothing. All the great treasures the Church has given us — the sacraments themselves, the Holy Scriptures, the gifts of the Holy Spirit, the sacramentals to sanctify the world — all those good things are channels of grace.

But all of them flow out from and come back to the Holy Eucharist, because that is Our Lord Himself — the Christ, the whole Christ, and nothing but the Christ.

We are to match His presence with ours. We are to complete His presence with ours. Our Lord is in the Blessed Sacrament regardless of us. Our faith doesn't put Him there. His being there puts us in faith. We believe because He is there.

We should always be responding to His presence with *our* presence. *Our goal and desire should be to live within the Sacred Heart of Jesus.* Always. We can make our responding presence to Jesus in His Holy Eucharist more real by visiting Him in the Tabernacle or adoration chapel often, by invoking Him in prayer throughout the day, by thanking Him for giving us Himself so that we can be with Him for all eternity.

Please don't count on the Poor Clares, the Carmelites, or the Trappists to do this for you—the cloistered religious who spend their days and nights in prayer before the Blessed Sacrament. They live an extraordinary life every day in prayer before the Lord. That is their beautiful vocation, to respond to Our Lord's presence by their presence in an endless dialogue with Him.

But *we are called by Him, too,* as much as our vocations will permit. The Lord shouldn't be left alone in our churches and chapels. True, He is never really left totally alone because He has His angels. There are enough angels to go around to every Tabernacle in the world.

But He wants us! He did not make His Holy Eucharist for the angels. The Eucharist is ours, and Our Lord waits for us and expects us to come visit Him when He is alone in the Tabernacle or the monstrance in an adoration chapel. He yearns for our live bodies to be present visiting Him, kneeling in prayer.

We must respond to Our Lord's invitation and His Real Presence here with us. There is a tremendous grace being offered to us by Him, if only we would make the time to visit Him in His earthly house, the Tabernacle.

Mass to Mass, Communion to Communion, there is no substitute for this on earth. *"Would that you would come visit me more often in my house,"* the Lord asks of us.

We as Catholics need Eucharistic Adoration, the private holy hours we make and the public Benedictions of the Most Blessed Sacrament in our churches and chapels. But, sad to say, promotion of Adoration today by many of our priests and pastors may seem to be but an indulgent gesture to the "old days" when formal public worship of the Blessed Sacrament was such a prominent fixed feature in every parish calendar:

Benediction at least every week, First Friday every month, the Forty Hours' Devotion every year. Now, however, we may be told by some "modern Catholics" that in the Brave New Church of the present and future, these are hopelessly outmoded manners of prayer.

This view of the traditional Eucharistic devotions of the Church may be the view of some clergy and members of the laity, but it is *not* the view of the Church herself. Devotion to the Eucharistic Christ is not, for the Catholic Church, some sop to sentiment, some pious luxury. No! It is of the essence of her life and mission. Without the Presence of her Lord in His chosen Sacrament in her midst, the Church would literally disappear; she would be nothing.

What we are doing here is not looking *back*, but looking *forward*. We are looking forward to what is *before* us, here and now, in solid reality—the reality of the Mystery of Faith in its absolute essentials, as revealed by God through His Son Jesus Christ, and as believed and taught by His Holy Catholic Church. This Mystery of Faith is essentially—and in a sense, uniquely and totally—this one thing: the Blessed Sacrament of the Altar, the Holy Eucharist.

The truth of the centrality and totality of the Eucharist is one of the clearest and most emphatic teachings of the Second Vatican Council. There is surely no need to prove this by quoting from any of a score of Conciliar texts. Now it is true that what the Council is stressing is Mass and Holy Communion—the Eucharist, as it were, in "action." The purpose of the Sacrament is what Vatican II stresses, namely, the gift to God and the communion with us; the sacrificial offering and the holy banquet, whereby Our Lord is united simultaneously with His Father and with mankind.

Yes, that is true. In fact, that is equally true of the Council of Trent, or of any other event or statement of the teaching Church concerning this subject. For such was indeed the intention of Christ, an intention expressly manifested by His institution: with its words indicating immolation, and its elements indicating food. Vatican II was therefore totally faithful to the unchanging Faith of the Church in reaffirming as it did the absolute primacy of this indivisible two-fold action of the Eucharist — the two-fold action which we call Holy Mass and Holy Communion.

ALIVE IN THE TABERNACLE

It is likewise true that the Second Vatican Council did not stress, in any proportionate manner, that other and secondary aspect of the Holy Eucharist, namely, its being reserved in the Tabernacle outside the time of Mass and actual Holy Communion. This reservation — or "repose" — of the Blessed Sacrament, which dates back to the earliest age of the Church, is in itself no hindrance to, nor distraction from, the "action" of the Blessed Sacrament. How could it be? Every consecrated Host was, after all, once offered in a Mass, and will eventually be received in a Holy Communion.

This enduring, "permanent" aspect of the Eucharist was adequately recognized by the Council; it endorsed and encouraged the devotion of the faithful toward the reserved Sacrament which in the course of the Church's centuries has steadily grown, both in depth of awareness and in breadth of expression. We need but mention such things as Benediction and the Forty Hours' Devotion and the solemnity of Corpus Christi, to appreciate what this Eucharistic devotion has meant — and continues to mean — to the Christian people.

If this secondary aspect of the Eucharist — this aspect of its repose — is thus clearly subordinated to its primary aspect — the aspect of its action — and if this subordination is thus clearly confirmed by Vatican II, then why may we not consider these Eucharistic devotions as no more than "fringe benefits," as a laudable but optional "extra," like any other devotion in the great "supermarket" of Catholic piety? The reason why we may not — and cannot — should be evident from the experience of these past decades since Vatican II.

What is this experience? Simply this: the *neglect* (I will not say the positive downgrading, as has been known to happen) — simply the neglect, the ignoring — of the worship of the Blessed Sacrament in the Tabernacle has eventually, or inevitably, led to the neglect, the ignoring, of the worship of the Blessed Sacrament in the Mass and in Holy Communion. (And you must remember that when we cease to worship Christ in the Sacrament, we cease to worship the Father through Christ, for the two are not two but one worship!)

Has the dropping of Benediction added to the attendance at Mass? We need not look at the difference in mere numbers, important as that is, for we have often been told how the numbers of Communions have actually increased.

But we can look at *how* the Mass is attended and *how* Communion is received. And from the general comportment of these same Catholic people, from Mass to Mass and from Communion to Communion, we can surely make some surmise about why there is a "crisis of faith" in the Church today!

No, the interaction of the interior and the exterior is not all that surprising or mysterious. If it is true that historically we Catholics have genuflected to the Blessed Sacrament because we believe in the Real Presence, is it not at least equally true that now, psychologically, we genuflect to the Blessed Sacrament to help us continue believing in the Real Presence? And if we no longer genuflect—or do any of the other practices sanctioned by the custom of the Church regarding the Blessed Sacrament on the altar—how much longer will we really believe?

This brings me to a yet deeper reason why devotion to the reserved Sacrament in the Tabernacle is in plain fact *necessary* if we are to preserve and increase our faith in the action of this same Sacrament in Mass and Holy Communion. And that is that the Mass and Holy Communion are immediately and specifically just that: Christ's *actions*. That is to say: they are not simply His Body and His Blood, but His Body as *broken* and His Blood as *poured out*—and as such offered to His Father in sacrifice, and to His brethren in communion.

But this "broken-ness" and this "poured-out-ness" are *in* His Body and His Blood. And His Body and Blood, in turn since they are Risen and living, are *in* His Soul and His Divinity. In other words, Christ *acts* in the Holy Eucharist only because He *is in* the Holy Eucharist. His *action* follows His *being*. And that being—necessary and unmistakable, but in a sense only indirect and "by concomitance," in the Mass and Communion—becomes direct and explicit as we contemplate the Blessed Sacrament in repose. Here in our midst is the Real Presence of the Being of Jesus Christ, exactly as real as He is in Heaven, and nowhere else as real on earth as He is right here.

It is the Real Presence of the Lord, in the Church's defined sense of the "real absence" of the bread and wine. It is this true, real and substantial Presence which ultimately and uniquely verifies the "Real Action" of Christ whereby He goes to His Father and abides with us. And what verifies the Real Presence? Does our faith verify it? No! He is there, whether we believe it or not.

WE DEPEND ON HIS PRESENCE

Our faith is dependent on His Presence. And so His Real Presence is dependent upon and is verified by Himself alone: by His power and His promise, by His provision of the priesthood, and ultimately by the unutterable mystery of His love.

It is true, literally true, that in a primary sense Christ in the Holy Eucharist *makes* the Church. For without His Action there is no communication of life, and without His Presence there is no life to communicate. Yet, in a secondary sense, it is true to say that Christ in the Holy Eucharist *is made* by the Church, for without the action of her ministers in Sacred Orders His Presence would not be effected. He would not be there as He wills to be, at once hidden and revealed by the sacramental sign.

This sacramental sign—these sacred species—should hereafter be more, not less, before you, all of you of the faithful laity. But you must ask the bishops who have the plenitude of the priesthood which makes them immediately responsible to Christ for the handling of His Body. Let us leave the bishops, then, with their responsibility—in the hands of Christ.

So too, in those same hands are to be placed all His priests: the men whom He has eternally sealed to bear His Person. For you, the laity, you must ask your priests to make the Body of Christ more available to you for Adoration and Benediction. What is happening in the Church now is an enormous *challenge*. Hackneyed as that word may be, it yet contains a reality. And that reality is now before you, as grim or as gleaming as it can be. It is a challenge which will open up to you new and undreamed of heights and depths of this Eucharistic mystery. But you must pray that your priests will help make it so that the Body of Christ is more available to you for Adoration in your parishes.

Your prayers in Adoration must be your own, in the private chamber of your heart and soul and addressed to the Father and Our Lord Jesus in secret. But your prayers must also carry over from your time in Adoration to the community of your family and your parish and your other associations of prayer, such as the Knights of Columbus, the Society of St. Vincent de Paul, third order religious fraternities, and parish prayer and Bible study groups.

In private and in public, by day and by night, you must *pray* the prayer of faith. Since faith depends upon His Presence (and not vice versa), your prayer must be *His* prayer—His Eucharistic Action in your frequent, even daily, Mass and Holy Communion. But do not forget that He has as well a Eucharistic Repose! That too is His prayer, and to share in it most intimately and enduringly, in public and in private by night and by day, *He invites you.*

As I trust we have seen in these brief reflections on the total Mystery of Faith that is the Holy Eucharist, the reservation of Our Lord's Presence in the Blessed Sacrament—and the prayer that is proper to it—is not a sentiment, a luxury, looking to the past. Rather, it is a reality, a necessity, looking to the future.

And well that it is so! For in this present time and in the times that can be foreseen, it will be *that prayer*, that prayer of

His Repose, which will sustain you, and all His Church. For here in the reserved Sacrament, whether hidden in the Tabernacle or exposed on the altar in a monstrance, is the Lord Jesus Christ in His repose! This is the repose of His majesty and His lowliness that alone can sustain, and will sustain, strongly yet serenely, patiently yet with joyful confidence and expectation, His faithful people.

O Sacrament most holy,
O Sacrament divine,
All praise and all thanksgiving,
Be every moment Thine!

REFLECTIONS FROM THE SAINTS

"You wanted to stay with us, and so you left us yourself in the Sacrament of the Altar, and you opened wide your mercy to us. You opened an inexhaustible spring of mercy for us, giving us your dearest possession, the Blood and Water, that gushed forth from your Heart." —ST. FAUSTINA KOWALSKA

"The Church and the world have a great need for Eucharistic worship. Jesus awaits us in this sacrament of love. Let us not refuse the time to go to meet Him in Adoration." —POPE ST. JOHN PAUL II

"Men will surrender to the spirit of the age. They will say that if they had lived in our day, faith would be simple and easy. But in their day, they will say things are complex; the Church must be brought up to date and made meaningful to today's problems." —ST. ANTHONY OF PADUA

"Do you realize that Jesus is there in the Tabernacle expressly for you—for you alone? He burns with the desire to come into your heart.... He does not come down from Heaven each day to stay in the gold chalice. He comes down to find another Heaven He cherishes infinitely more than the first, the Heaven of our souls, made in His image, living temples of the Most Blessed Trinity." —ST. THÉRÈSE OF LISIEUX

"Jesus has made Himself the Bread of Life to give us life. Night and day, He is there. If you really want to grow in love, come back to the Eucharist, come back to that Adoration." —ST. THERESA OF CALCUTTA

"One of the most admirable effects of Holy Communion is to preserve the soul from sin, and to help those who fall through weakness to rise again." —ST. IGNATIUS LOYOLA

"Let everyone be struck with fear, let the whole world tremble, and let the heavens exult when Christ, the Son of the living God, is present on the altar in the hands of a priest.... Brothers and sisters, behold the humility of God and pour out yourselves before Him! Humble yourselves that you may be exalted by Him! Hold back nothing of yourselves for yourselves, so that He Who gives Himself totally to you may receive you totally." —ST. FRANCIS OF ASSISI

CHAPTER FIVE

EUCHARISTIC REFLECTIONS

"He had always loved those who were His in the world, but now He showed how perfect His love was" (Jn 13:1).

WHY IS IT THAT OF ALL THE CHANGES, OR talk of changes, in our Catholic religion since Vatican Council II in the 1960s, none have caused more deep division of thought and feeling among us than those which have touched on the Holy Eucharist? This kind of division is, of course, nothing new for the Holy Church. For centuries Christians have been divided over the meaning or the practices following from the meaning of this sacrament. This is all the more tragic when we remember that this sacrament was instituted by Our Lord to be not only the sign but the cause of unity: unity with Himself and unity among all His members. The Eucharist was meant to be our peace, the source and very substance of our peace. Yet see the strife which it has occasioned! What are we to make of this tragic fact?

First, we must remember that if there is a providence in everything (and there certainly is, for *nothing* happens without God's allowance), there is a special providence of God regarding His Eucharist. The very fact that it should seem to be the source of division and contention, of anything but peace and unity, that very fact should remind us that the Holy Eucharist is indeed important! It does make a difference! It cannot be ignored!

God is allowing the Blessed Sacrament to be the occasion of our misery: to force us to consider it—and ourselves—again, to prevent us from ever again taking it for granted. If nothing had happened concerning this sacrament in the late Twentieth Century, how often would we now be thinking of it? God's ways are indeed mysterious; but this is not the first time that He has brought good out of the evil that He has allowed.

When we recall the circumstances of its institution, this thought about a special providence concerning the Holy Eucharist becomes very clear indeed. Did not Our Lord institute this sacrament in the very context of a *betrayal*? Is it not in its very essence the Memorial of His Passion? Was there total peace and unity even at the Last Supper, when a traitor sat among his fellow Apostles, and they sat bewildered and troubled in heart?

Thus, even from the very beginning, the Holy Eucharist was a sign of contradiction. And, indeed, ought we not to have expected it to be so, since it *is* Christ (cf. Lk 2:34)? *His* peace and *His* unity are there, but they are hidden—safely and serenely changeless beyond all the changes that surround His sign.

As for ourselves, then, let us thank Him for *all*—yes, even for our past sins of faithlessness, even our treacheries. For now, aware at last of our misery, we can be truly changed by this special providence of His changelessness: our divisions, our contentions can be changed into His unity and peace. This is what His Eucharist can do—and will do—if we but let Him do so, by our coming again and yet again to Him in this, His chosen sign.

EMMANUEL—GOD IS WITH US

When we speak of the Holy Eucharist as "it," we must, of course, immediately remind ourselves that that kind of language is totally inadequate to express the reality of what "it" in very fact is. The Eucharist is indeed a sacrament, and a sacrament is a sign, and a sign is a thing; and so in some sense we do refer to the Eucharist as "it."

But the reality—the total existent being—of this particular sign called "sacrament," and of this particular sacrament called "Eucharist," demands that we speak of it not as something but as some *one*. The sign as such, i.e., that which does the signing, may be "it"; but the reality which is signed is He. In its total reality, therefore, the Holy Eucharist is someone, the very Person of God Incarnate, Our Lord Jesus Christ.

There was a time not many years ago when the Real Presence of Christ in the Eucharist was a subject for controversy only with non-Catholics. For us Catholics it was the virtual substance—and therefore the surest sign—of our faith. To prevent any doubt that this is unchanged, that the Real Presence is as constitutive and designative of the Catholic Faith as it has always been, our late Holy Father Pope Paul VI issued a great encyclical, *Mysterium Fidei*. There he reaffirmed most categorically the traditional and solemnly defined faith of the Church: Jesus Christ is "truly, really, and substantially" present in the Eucharist, and thus totally present—His Body and Blood, Soul, and Divinity.

Moreover, He is present in the Eucharist not in the sense of His being in something, i.e., in the bread and the wine. For the bread and the wine, that were indeed there before Christ became present, are no longer there as substances, i.e., as things. Their total substance is changed by the power of God into the total substance of the Body and Blood of Christ. Corresponding to the real presence of Christ is the real absence of anything else. Not only is the Eucharist, therefore, totally Christ, it is *only* He.

This teaching of the Catholic Church concerning the total and exclusive reality of Christ's Eucharistic presence is called the doctrine of transubstantiation. This formidable term was historically adopted by the teaching Church, not as some kind of extra—as a help, for example, to explain our faith or stimulate our devotion. If that was the purpose, it has hardly succeeded, for the "Mystery of Faith" is still very much there, and our piety is not likely to be inspired by this rather unaesthetic term.

No, the Church adopted "transubstantiation"—and insists upon it—as something *essential*, i.e., as the best available term for situating the mystery, for expressing the sense of our faith. Anyone who claims to believe in a "real presence" which denies or doubts or even prescinds from transubstantiation, must know immediately that he is not a Catholic in this essential constituent of the one true Faith.

As the experience of centuries has amply proved, to reject transubstantiation is to reject the Real Presence; and to reject that is to reject the Holy Eucharist—for that is what "it" is.

"Holy Eucharist" or "Blessed Sacrament" or whatever other name we may use as drawn from the thought and prayer of the Church's tradition—these names designate, primarily and totally, not a thing but a person. He is there, upon the Church's altar, at once hidden and revealed by the appearances of the things He chose to sign Himself. But behind and in those appearances is totally and only He: Jesus Christ, fulfilling thus in utter truth His title of "Emmanuel—God with us."

LORD, TO WHOM SHALL WE GO?

When we say, as we commonly do, that the Holy Eucharist contains the Real Presence of Christ, we really mean that it *is* the Real Presence. The only "thing" there in the ciborium or monstrance on our altars is the Body of Christ. And since it is the only body He has, it is living, and therefore pulsating with His blood, and enlivened by His soul, and subsisting by his Divine person. This is the truth upon which the Catholic Church by solemn definition and constant teaching has staked her entire Faith.

No wonder, then, that there is wonder here! That there is even scandal! Why must the Church be so insistent on this "transubstantiation"? Why can't she leave all that aside, and tell us rather what Christ does in His Eucharist: how He gives us here the sign of His love, of His peace, of His sharing with the Father and with us? Why can't the Eucharist be the sign it was meant to be: pointing to something beyond it rather than to itself, being the means rather than the object of our worship? Don't we need to "feed in faith" rather than steep ourselves in "metaphysics" or in "magic"?

The answer to this scandalized wonder was already given us by Our Lord Himself when He asked His Apostles whether, on account of this hard saying, they also would turn and walk with Him no more. We should not be surprised, then, at this reaction; it is as old as the Gospel itself. Those who mistake faith for magic only prove that the faith they speak of as a "feeding" is still all too human, too rational to be truly from Heaven—the very gift of God. By faith which is truly from Heaven, we see that what is "signed" by the appearances of bread and wine is *not* love or peace or a sharing—in any immediate sense. Rather, what is "signed" is no more nor less than what Christ said it was: "This is my Body; this is my Blood."

Indeed, how can Christ *do* anything in His Eucharist unless antecedently He is in it? First discern by faith the Body of the Lord as being there and then you will see what that Body can do and is doing here! His peace, His love, His unity can only be for those who believe in Him. He cannot lead us to the Father unless He first draws us to Himself. He has come down as Bread from Heaven for the life of the world. Reflecting on the full sweep of this mystery, we see that the world cannot have this life until it first recognizes this Bread for what it is.

Transubstantiation is neither metaphysics nor magic. It is *mystery*! It is the mystery of faith, or perhaps better still: the mystery of *the* Faith. This mystery is indeed related to love, and intrinsically so in a twofold way: it is caused by love, and it causes love. God's love for us causes Him to be this Eucharist, and His being this Eucharist causes us to love Him in return.

But in the center of this love is the one Eucharistic being: the living Body and Blood of the Lord. And He from His Eucharist asks us in our turn: "Will you also go away?" We can only answer: "Lord, to whom shall we go? You have the words of eternal life" (Jn 6:67–68).

RE-PRESENTING HIS SACRIFICE

If Our Lord Jesus Christ, in the totality of His living Person, is the Holy Eucharist (and that, by defined Catholic Faith, is all and only what the Eucharist is), He is so because He intends to do something by means of this new manner of His existence.

Therefore, it is quite true that the Eucharist must always be seen by us as it has always been seen by our fathers in the Faith: not only as an end in itself, the object indeed of the same adoration that we give to God alone, but also as a means whereby we fulfill the purpose of our being—to love the Lord our God with all our hearts and our neighbor as ourselves. In fact, the Eucharist is not just a means to this fulfillment; it is *the* means. For is it not the means whereby Christ Himself fulfilled His purpose in coming into the world—to love God His Father and us with the one total love of His Heart?

He fulfilled that purpose and that commandment in His Paschal Mystery: His death and resurrection. And isn't the Holy Eucharist in its institution and essence nothing but this: His Paschal Mystery rendered perpetually present, until He comes again?

How does Our Lord love His Father and us by means of the Holy Eucharist? By *re-presenting* His Sacrifice—His death upon the cross. His lifted Body is re-presented by the sign of bread to be broken, and His shed Blood is re-presented by the sign of wine to be poured.

Loving His Father and us is what He does right now as much as He did then, for it is His Sacrifice right now as much as it was then; the one same Heart's love, the one same Sacrifice. And we consume the broken bread and the poured wine as food, for His sacrificed Body and Blood are our life whereby we in our turn are enabled to love God our Father and all men our brothers. This life for which we were made—and without which we are dead—is nowhere given us as it is in the Mass and Holy Communion of the Eucharistic Christ (cf. Jn 6:53).

The Holy Eucharist, then, is *the* means of Christ's life and our own; in it He completes His resurrection, and in it we anticipate ours. But, once again, not in spite of the Eucharist being this means, but precisely because it is such, is it not all the clearer now why the ancient and enduring "sense of the Faith" leads us to adore in itself this Mystery of the Faith? We can do what we are here in this world to do—to love God and for God our neighbor—only because Jesus is doing this same thing before us. And He is *doing* it only because He *is* here.

Is our love for God and neighbor "distracted" by our adverting to the Eucharistic Presence of Jesus Christ? In turning to Him as the object of our gaze, are we being "turned aside" from the fulfillment of our life's commandment? The question answers itself. Unless we see Him as He has chosen to be seen, namely in His Eucharistic sign, we cannot see God or man as they are, namely in Christ.

HIS SACRIFICE AND OURS

By means of the Holy Eucharist, as we have seen, Our Lord Jesus Christ fulfills His mission in this world: He perpetuates to the end of time and space the one cumulative act of His life, namely, the gift of His life to His Father in His death. It is in this sense that the Eucharist is essentially the memorial of His Passion. What Christ does, therefore, is simply go to His Father. He thus completes the circuit, as it were, whereby He came from the Father—from eternity as His consubstantial Word, into time as this same Word made flesh.

This "going to the Father" has been traditionally called in the theology and piety of the Church the *sacrifice* of Christ. And because it is His sacrifice, it is strictly the only sacrifice. That is to say, it is the only action in the entire history of mankind which actually accomplished just that: going to the Father—or, in other words, becoming one with God—or, again in other words, being made a holy thing (*sacrum facere*).

All other actions that have been called sacrifices are really such only by analogy, i.e., only insofar as they are related to this one action, this one sacrifice of Christ. This is clearly the meaning of such diverse sacrifices as Abel's and Abraham's and Melchizedek's and the official cult of the Jerusalem temple. Both the offerers and the offered in all these instances were "made holy" (i.e., were a sacrifice) only because they referred in some figurative way to the unique Holy One, at once Priest and Victim: the Christ.

Now, just as His giving of Himself to the Father (which is His love) was represented by His death, and just as the external event of death is valueless without the internal reality of love, so too His death is represented—made visible—for all time and space by the sacrament He instituted on the eve of that death.

Without Calvary the Eucharist would not only cease to be a sacrifice, it would cease to be anything; for its only reality is the broken Body and the poured-out Blood of the Lord. Likewise, without the Eucharist, Calvary would lose the unique value and significance given it by Our Lord Himself. It would remain an historic event, no doubt, even an objective instance of heroic love. Yet it would no longer have either the immediacy or the universality—the total gathering up of all mankind into holiness, into oneness with God—that the demands of His love intended it to be.

The Mass—i.e., the Eucharist as sacrifice—is the source, the center, and summation of the Christian religion. For it alone makes us holy, it alone makes us to be one with God ("at-onement"). It is the only and total action of the *totus Christus*: Jesus Christ, with and in the members of His Mystical Body, going to His Father.

"Love," "the Cross," "the Mass": these three terms have but one identical meaning and value, namely, the life of Jesus giving and given to His Father, for our life: His sacrifice and ours.

A SACRIFICE OR A MEAL?

Next to the confusion regarding what the Holy Eucharist is (namely, the total and exclusive reality of the Body and Blood of Christ), there is none sadder nor more ominous than the consequent confusion among many Catholics regarding what the Eucharist does—or, in some related sense, what we are to do with it.

This confusion is vividly evidenced by the current controversy as to whether the Holy Eucharist is a sacrifice or a meal. The fact that it is both—indeed, that it has to be both if it is to be either!—seems to have become obscured in the minds of all too many among us. If the Eucharist-as-Sacrifice is, as we have seen, simply Christ's going to His Father, doesn't it follow that, since He wills to go thither in His whole Body, He must come into us—i.e., be the Eucharist-as-Meal? And conversely, if the Eucharist-as-Meal is His coming into us, doesn't it follow that where He is we also are—i.e., with His Father, in the Eucharist-as-Sacrifice?

This absolute solidarity between the sacrifice and the meal—between Mass and Holy Communion—is thus based on the absolute unity of the Eucharist itself as being Christ's living Body: His one Body, Head and members together in the one love of His Heart.

This unity has been emphasized by the Church in our time, and changes in her discipline have made it progressively more realizable by the individual members. However, she hasn't said—nor will she ever say—that the individual member's assistance at Mass has no value nor even meaning unless that person also receives Holy Communion at that Mass. Nor will the Church say that the reception of Holy Communion outside of Mass is no longer permissible. In other words, these two "moments" of the Eucharist, for all their intrinsic solidarity, still remain distinct and even separable. The role of the celebrant alone is and will be—as it has always been—the essential minimum for the "doing" of the Eucharist. The priest alone at the altar effects this unity of sacrifice and meal, just as he alone effects the reality of the presence on which the reality of both sacrifice and meal is based.

But what are we to say about Holy Communion, this Eucharist-as-Meal? Are we in this present "renewal" of the Church really aware of what we do when we approach this "table," when we handle this "bread," when we consume it? Do we realize that unlike ordinary bread, which is changed into ourselves, this Bread changes us into itself? This Bread does indeed change us into itself if we recognize it for what it is, if we discern it to be the very Body of the Lord.

Perhaps the current casualness about this Bread is explained by the fact that we do *not* discern the Body (cf. 1 Cor 11:29). On this discernment, then, depends the possibility of our ever being truly changed into Christ. On it depends the possibility of the Church's ever being truly renewed. On it depends, for us who have been invited to this Meal, the very possibility of our not dying of *surfeited hunger*.

And that gift is man's for as long as the world endures. The Eucharist is Holy Thursday, Good Friday, and Easter Sunday all wrapped into one supreme act of giving and loving on the part of the Son of God.

THE POWER OF THE HOLY SPIRIT

The Holy Eucharist, as we have seen, is the very person of Our Lord Jesus Christ as "signed" by the elements and actions He instituted, whereby He continues to do in all time and space what He did once for all in His Paschal Mystery; give Himself to His Father (in Sacrifice) and give Himself to us (in Communion).

This is the very substance of the "Mystery of Faith"; in it all our faith (and our life) is contained—or, if you wish to say it more dynamically, into it and out of it all our faith (and our life) moves.

But now there remains one further essential aspect of this Mystery which we have not yet considered, and which is in fact all too often neglected, with the result that the living unity of our Catholic Faith is imperiled. How can we keep in living unity that which is visible ("institutional") and that which is invisible ("charismatic") in what we believe? Our Lord, Who in His Divinity from eternity and in His humanity since His ascension is invisible to us, is now made visible by the same unique Cause that made Him visible in His incarnation, namely, the Holy Spirit!

Just as the Holy Spirit is the Cause of the incarnation ("He was made flesh by the Holy Spirit"), so is He the Cause of the

Eucharist ("We believe in the Holy Spirit, the Lord and Giver of life"). Jesus is "the Christ" because He was "anointed" by the Holy Spirit: an anointing (a "christening"!) whereby a created human nature in the very instant of its creation not only *had* the divine life but *was* the Divine Life, in the one Person of the Son of God.

The Holy Spirit, therefore, is the Cause of Jesus' being the God-Man. He is also, therefore, the Cause of this God-Man's actions—and especially of this God-Man's action *par excellence*: His Paschal Mystery. That is why the Holy Spirit is mentioned in all the Eucharistic Prayers of our renewed liturgy as being the *Cause of holiness*: making holy our gifts (so that they can become Christ's Body and Blood) and making *us* holy (so that we can become Christ's members in His Body and Blood).

This power of the Holy Spirit, of which the sign (both as cause and as effect) is the Holy Eucharist, builds the Church in all her aspects—as individuals and as a community, as institutional and as charismatic—into the life and unity which is God. Only the Spirit can search and comprehend this Mystery, which is itself the Spirit (1 Cor 2:10–11)! Only by our participation in the Holy Eucharist (in reality or at least in desire) are we put, as it were, within the "circuit" of the Holy Spirit.

And the same one Person who—in diverse ways—makes Father and Son to be one God, and Divinity and humanity to be one Christ, and our human gifts and the divine Gift to be one Eucharist, and the visible and invisible to be one Church, makes all and each of us to be "one spirit"—in Him (1 Cor 6:17).

In Eucharistic adoration, it is not that worthless "self" that we exhibit to Our Lord. Before Our Lord, that "self" shrinks to its proper nothingness. (Is that why there are so few adorers?) It is the power and the love and infinite goodness of the Eucharistic Lord that come to fill our nothingness with the very "fullness of God."

If all we have to share with our neighbor are our own thoughts or desires or opinions or feelings we offer a *nothing*.

But if Our Lord fills our mind and will and heart every moment of our lives—then it is the "fullness of God" we share with others, without any diminution of our own interior life.

THE FIRST TABERNACLE HERE ON EARTH

Almost as important as the fact of the Holy Spirit's being the cause of the Eucharist (and we have already seen that He is the cause) is the manner of His causing it. He causes it not as Creator but as "re-Creator." For He chooses to use a pre-existing creature—an effect of His previous creation—from which He draws the material of His new creation.

The creature in the proximate instance of the Holy Eucharist is, of course, the bread and wine—"which earth has given and human hands have made." But in its fundamental instance, does not the Eucharist presuppose another creature, immeasurably more fundamental in its elemental nature and in its human cooperation, and thus immeasurably more commensurate with what the Holy Spirit will effect from it? As the very culmination of the "first creation"—last in the order of nature and first in the order of grace—the fundamental matter of the Eucharist is the same as the fundamental matter of the incarnation itself, for these two realities are the same one "new creation": the Christ, born of "the Woman," the New Eve: Mary Immaculate.

As especially sung of in the Christmas liturgy, what a *commercium* (i.e., an exchange) was here! The Son of God, by the power of His Spirit, takes on our mortality, and gives us His immortality in return; our nature becomes God's nature, and His nature becomes ours! Yet neither nature is lost or merged in the exchange. They are distinct, though inseparable, in the Holy Spirit.

And the perfect fulfillment of this exchange is Mary, His perfect creature. Alone of all creatures, she was twice created by Him in the same one instant of time: created in nature and recreated in grace, in her one Immaculate Conception. What a *commercium* indeed is this affirmation of our Catholic Faith: that we should see the source of our first earthly nature in the immediate uncreated action from Heaven of the Spirit of God, and the source of our second heavenly nature (namely, grace) in the created cooperative receptivity on earth of Blessed Mary!

Now all this truth of the Catholic Faith is not an abstraction, a matter of words buried in books somewhere. No, it is alive, this Mystery of Faith; it is a living, physical reality, a Word at once totally divine and totally human, reserved in the Tabernacles of our churches. These Tabernacles we adorn as best we can, since they contain the same identical reality that is adored in Heaven.

These Tabernacles should remind us of that original Tabernacle, first here on earth and now assumed into Heaven: the body and soul of Mary Immaculate, first Mother of God and now Mother of the Church. No wonder that our devotion to her has always been and will always be the exact measure of our devotion to the Holy Eucharist—and vice versa. No wonder, also, that these two devotions, which God Himself by His Holy Spirit has made inseparable, *are the one sure sign of the Catholic faith*. If we have one of them, we have them both—and we have all (for we are "Catholic"!). But lose one of them, and both are lost—and *all* is lost.

LET US THANK HIM

After considering Our Blessed Lady, these Eucharistic reflections turn to those "twelve times twelve thousand," whose serried ranks complete in Heaven the glorious Body of Christ. The blessed saints—our elder brothers and sisters who have preceded us into eternity, and whose intercession and example help us toward joining them there—must never be dissociated from our devotion to the Blessed Sacrament.

Just as the Eucharistic Christ is integral to our Marian devotion, so is He to our devotion to the saints. For is not the Eucharist the source and summit of the Christian life, as Vatican II has reminded us? Is it not therefore the very summation of their sanctity: this one unique and total sanctity of Jesus Christ, in this one unique and total Mystery of His love?

It is surely no coincidence, then, that in the Creed the one reference to the saints contains the Eucharistic word "communion." The communion of saints *is* Holy Communion! Receiving the Body of Christ is not just our *way* to Heaven; it is *already* our Heaven! The saints in glory have no more, essentially, than what we have right now on earth. The reality of the divine life—the sanctifying grace that is Jesus—fills Heaven, Earth, and Purgatory. The only place where it is definitely absent is Hell; and that absence is what defines Hell. Although this divine life is viewed in different ways, it is nevertheless one: the one only Catholic Church, the one only Bride and Body of Christ.

We are fortunate to be living in this age of the conciliar Church, for surely this reality of communion in its richest and dearest sense has never been more realizable than right now. In two distinct but complementary senses this is true. First, there is now the opportunity of greater actual communion among more of the baptized members of Christ than ever before. Thanks to the great disciplinary changes of the last century—St. Pius X's regarding children, and St. Paul VI's regarding certain non-Catholic Christians—Holy Communion is more accessible, hence more commensurate with its potential as the cause and sign of all grace.

Yet at the same time, this very openness prompts us to become more aware of what this Communion demands of us: faith and charity. This Sacrament of the Living presupposes in us the state of grace as much as it increases in us that state of grace. Remember those two seemingly irreconcilable details in Our Lord's parable of the supper: on the one hand, his servants are to bring into the marriage feast as many as they can find; on the other hand, his servants are to cast into outer darkness whoever has come in without a wedding garment (cf. Mt 22:9, 12–13)!

These two points are really not irreconcilable, but complementary. They reflect the same one reality of the Church, which is at once the unique and sinless Bride and the all-embracing Mother of sinners. They likewise reflect the same one reality of

Christ, Who is at once the All-Holy and Sole-Begotten One and the Suffering Servant and First-Born from the Dead.

So, if it is true that the scandal of contradiction is in these our times not less but more, it is also true that that very scandal is the sign of Christ (cf. Lk 2:34)—and preeminently so in this, His supreme and ultimate sign: His Holy Eucharist (cf. Mt 26:31).

Let us therefore conclude these reflections on the Holy Eucharist where we began them: by thanking Him amid the scandal of betrayal, for the very word Eucharist means thanks, and it was first given on the night He was betrayed. Let us thank Him for this "extremism" of His life, whereby He betrayed Himself into becoming our Emanuel in Person—loving us "unto the end" (Jn 13:1).

REFLECTIONS FROM THE SAINTS

"Jesus, You come to me and unite Yourself intimately to me in the form of nourishment. Your Blood now runs in mine. Your Soul, Incarnate God, compenetrates mine, giving courage and support. What miracles! Who would have ever imagined such?"—ST. MAXIMILIAN KOLBE

"My Heart overflows with great mercy for souls, and especially for poor sinners. If only they could understand that I am the best of Fathers to them and that it is for them that the Blood and Water flowed from My Heart as from a fount overflowing with mercy. For them I dwell in the Tabernacle as King of Mercy. I desire to bestow My graces upon souls, but they do not want to accept them. You, at least, come to Me as often as possible and take these graces they do not want to accept. In this way you will console My Heart. Oh, how indifferent are souls to so much goodness, to so many proofs of love! My Heart drinks only of the ingratitude and forgetfulness of souls living in the world. They have time for everything, but they have no time to come to Me for graces."—JESUS TO ST. MARIA FAUSTINA KOWALSKA

"Do you want the Lord to give you many graces? Visit Him often. Do you want Him to give you few graces? Visit Him rarely. Do you want the devil to attack you? Visit Jesus rarely in the Blessed Sacrament. Do you want the devil to flee from you? Visit Jesus often!"—ST. JOHN BOSCO

"Even a quarter of an hour's prayer in front of the Eucharist perhaps gains more graces than all the other spiritual exercises of the day." —ST. ALPHONSUS LIGUORI

"A Holy Hour helps the one in the world in most need of God's Mercy.... Our Holy Hours of Eucharistic Adoration make us more sensitive to the needs of our fellow man. Eucharistic Adoration is an invaluable conversation with Christ where we learn more deeply of the mysteries of His Divine and human life." —POPE ST. JOHN PAUL II

"Every Holy Hour we make so pleases the Heart of Jesus that it is recorded in Heaven and retold for all eternity. Jesus has made Himself the Bread of Life to give us life. Night and day, He is there. If you really want to grow in love, come back to the Eucharist, come back to that Adoration." —ST. THERESA OF CALCUTTA

"A thousand years of enjoying human glory is not worth even an hour spent sweetly communing with Jesus in the Blessed Sacrament." —ST. PADRE PIO

CHAPTER SIX

INTERIOR RENEWAL: THE KEY TO A LIFE IN CHRIST

"Do not model yourselves on the behavior of the world around you, but let your behavior change, modelled by your new mind. This is the only way to discover the will of God and know what is good, what it is that God wants, what is the perfect thing to do" (Rom 12:2).

THERE ARE TOO MANY SIGNS OF AN immense grace from Heaven simply awaiting a response from our hearts. Can we see these occasions of grace and respond to them? The Holy Mass of full Paschaltime, wherein therefore the Risen Christ is especially present, in the opening to us of the Scriptures, and in the breaking of the bread, is a gift to us from God unlike any other. Within the heavenly aureole of the Holy Mass, let us briefly reflect on the Providential import of what God has given us.

The work of Catholics today is to support, defend, and advance the efforts of the teaching Church. But this work we are called to must be seen within the perspective of the Second Vatican Council, for that is the teaching Church of our times. Now, since that Council declared that its primary—if not its exclusive—theme was that of "renewal," we must strive ever better to understand what this renewal means. Especially so, since it is quite painfully clear how renewal has been misunderstood through these recent years, with the result that the authentic renewal called for by the Council is all the more urgent now, more even than it was when the Council first made that call.

What is this authentic renewal? Most simply yet most adequately put, it is that renewal which is *interior*—the renewal of our hearts. This change of heart—or *metanoia*—is the heart of the New Testament (cf. Ezek 36).

And since the New Testament is also the Eternal Testament, in itself it cannot be changed; it can only be *renewed*. That is why the Council sanctioned changes in the Church only insofar as they would clearly and unmistakably help this *one* change within us—helping, that is, either by disposing us for this change of heart, or by channeling the action that would flow from it. We must therefore work on this interior renewal, this renewal of our hearts, if we are to "renew the New Testament"—if we are to follow the teaching Church in her Council, if we are to be faithful to the Faith in which and for which we are united as Catholics.

The faith of the New Testament is, of course, identified with faith in Jesus Christ as already come among us and living in us the renewal of His Paschal Mystery. The whole of the Faith is contained in this one Mystery: "Christ has died, Christ is risen, Christ will come again." Everything is contained here because God so wills it: our destiny is to be with God as His children in Heaven, united with His one Child, the Eternal Son.

This union with Jesus is effected first by His Death and Resurrection which is past, and then by our own death and resurrection which is to come. This past and this future meet in the present, in our faith in this Jesus Who is in His sacrament right now before us at every Mass and is then to be within us at Holy Communion.

This Jesus, as He Himself told us, is the Truth personified. The object of our believing is therefore Himself, His very Person. To Him, in Him, terminates the motion of my mind and heart—this motion which is my total turning from myself to Him. If our renewal has this nature of a total turning to Jesus from ourselves, it is clear what its manner must also be. It must be something very deep within us. Our very selves, unlocked from the dungeon of selfhood which is called *pride*, turns now to Jesus and goes to Him—or rather into Him, into His very Self—that Heart which is the exact opposite of the prison of pride. His Heart is the heaven of humility; and humility, as we should know, is but another name for Truth.

But now, this interior renewal thus briefly described is anything but "interior" in the sense of being exclusively subjective to myself alone. Jesus is "*my* Savior," yes; and my faith in Him is person-to-person and heart-to-heart. But this personal Jesus has willed from His Heart to effect this union with me by means of sacraments, which means, that is, *outward signs* within a *community*—which is His Church. I would not have the sacraments, then, unless I have the Church.

Nor would I have the Faith either, without the Church. For "faith comes by hearing" (Rom 10:17), and the Lord has chosen to speak to me and all the world through others' voices—the voices of His official witnesses, the Apostles and their successors. When I hear the Church speak, in the person of the bishops with the Holy Father, I hear Christ speak—the same one Christ Who, in the Person of the Holy Spirit, speaks within me of and to the Father.

Christ is not divided from His Church, because He cannot be divided from Himself. The Truth of His Person as the "author and finisher of faith" (Heb 12:2) is the beginning and the end and the identical summation of "the truths of the Faith" as believed and taught by the Catholic Church.

Perhaps the best single word to designate this total—or Catholic—Faith is that ancient word enshrined in the Roman Canon: "orthodoxy." Now, from what we have seen is it not clear that the key to orthodoxy is interior renewal? How can we better keep the Faith than by purifying our hearts and keeping them pure from sin—especially the sin of pride—and turned in the prayer of humility and total trust to the Heart of Christ?

And in that same humility and trust our hearts will be attentive to the voice of His Church: the Magisterium. Thus, we will keep always in mind our "catechism answers"—for they are the formulations of the Faith without which our personal faith in the Person of Christ becomes mute and eventually vanishes. Indeed, if we really ponder these formulations, if we make them *our own*, as the Church insists we do, we will soon enough see that, far from being some kind of countering tendency to the motion of our hearts, they reinforce that motion! And why should they not, if what we are speaking of here are not two different things—a subjective faith and an objective creed—but rather a single reality, with two aspects essentially correlative and complementary?

THE RENEWAL OF OUR HEARTS

Our interior renewal cannot be authentic unless it is orthodox. But our orthodoxy in and of itself (in the sense, that is, of its being identical with "faith alone") cannot avail unto salvation, for ourselves or for anyone else. (We must never forget that the Scribes and Pharisees were very "orthodox"!) No, salvation—union with God—comes only with grace and charity, and that comes only in the heart.

From this brief reflection we must conclude that the renewal of our hearts, far from being something irrelevant to orthodoxy or even possibly hostile to it, is in reality the key to orthodoxy—its most intrinsic ingredient and its surest guarantee.

This also means, therefore, that interior renewal is the key to success in our *catechetical* apostolate with others, since catechesis is the work, now so prominent in our post-conciliar times, by which orthodoxy is re-established, maintained, and strengthened among the members of the Church.

But what of the second great apostolate of our times, the one which actually precedes catechesis, by looking to those vast numbers of mankind who are not yet members of the Church, namely, Evangelization? Interior renewal may well be necessary, you may say, for such an internal work of the Church as catechesis, but is it really necessary for such an external work as evangelization?

If the Gospel were just another message of worldly salvation—of liberation from so-called "sinful structures" and the like—then of course there is no problem: the Gospel could be sold like any other commodity in the marketplace. But if the Gospel is literally something from Heaven and leading to Heaven, then there must be evidence of Heaven in its messengers. That means a detachment from this world and from self, and a total attachment to Christ. And Christ, of course, as He has willed to manifest Himself in our world, as identified with the least of His brethren.

Only by a heart purified from sin and selfishness and turned selflessly to the grace of Christ can the world come to recognize the Gospel for what it is: the Good News of the only true salvation.

Again, the relationship here is correlative and complementary. Just as I cannot really love my neighbor as he deserves unless I love the God Who made and remade him in His image, so too I cannot love this Creator and Redeemer God unless I love His work, His image, His little ones.

We need not fear, then, this turning from self as though it were a turning from God's whole creation. The self I turn from is rather *my* creation! And with self behind me, I will for the first time see what God has really made, and the goodness that He saw in it. And it will lead me through this very goodness to its one ultimate source, which is His Most Sacred Heart.

In these reflections, I have endeavored to show the primacy—if not the totality—of interior renewal as the "one thing necessary" (Lk 10:42), and in fact, in a certain sense, the "one thing possible" for us in this New and Eternal Testament of God's infinite love for us.

For what else, really, can we do but turn our hearts, our whole souls to Him? Oh, we can and we must do the works assigned to us in His Providence for our lives: our labors manual, intellectual, and moral, and our responsibilities familial, civic, and ecclesial. But all these labors and responsibilities are salvific only if done in the grace of Christ; and that grace is something we do not achieve or negotiate! We *receive* it! And receiving is, by definition, a suffering!

Does this not perhaps illumine the Mystery of which we spoke at the beginning—the Mystery of Faith? The Paschal Mystery of the Death and Resurrection of Our Lord is best summarized in His own words: "Ought not the Christ to have suffered, and so enter into His glory?" (Lk 24:26). Externally, Christ suffered at the hands of sinners, and so does His Church.

But far deeper and more mysterious than this is His *interior* suffering—and the interior suffering of His Church. This suffering is caused by what I may dare to call His burden of grace, His Cross of glory. He emptied Himself of all the attributes of His Divinity, except His love, which was now the more manifest in His poverty and lowliness—a lowliness wherein His humanity would receive the absolute fullness of the Holy Spirit.

Becoming Incarnate in emptiness, Christ Jesus is now in fullness the Redeemer! And this fullness, this *pleroma* of Pauline splendor, is now before us in the Holy Eucharist, and now surrounding us in the One, Holy, Catholic and Apostolic Church. Truth personified and Mercy Incarnate have their perfect sign in the sacraments and the Church—at once so hidden and so radiant, so lowly and so exalted, so wounded and so alive with the very life of God!

The Church of lowliness and suffering on earth and the Church of exaltation and perfect joy in Heaven are identically one Church—the one Bride of the one Bridegroom, Christ. To His perfected members, His blessed saints, let us now lift up our hearts. And immeasurably beyond all the saints—as closest to him and closest to us—is Blessed Mary Immaculate, Mother of God and Mother of the Church. Her total blessedness is explained by Our Lord Himself as consisting in the one simple fact that she heard the word of God and kept it (Lk 11:28). That Eternal Word she received as a seed and pondered in her heart—and she brought forth the Salvation of the world!

May we, too, not dare to bear Him, after the manner of His Mother? He bids us do just that! And therefore, we can! For before we bear Him, He bears us—His branches, His witnesses, His little ones—upon His shoulders, in His arms, close to His beating Heart.

WE ARE CALLED TO FOLLOW HIM

Our Lord reminds us in Paschaltime of that truth which we have so often paraphrased by saying that we, the disciples of Jesus, are to be *in* the world, yet we are not to be *of* the world. Paraphrase and paradox: this being simultaneously *in* yet not *of* the world is the perfect description of what Catholics should be as united for the Faith. Men and women living in the world by a natural vocation blessed by God the Creator, we are called out from this world by God the Redeemer to follow Him—in the Passion of His Passover, wherein He receives the world's hatred and turns it back into love.

And in and by this very love—which *is* God the Sanctifier—we unite our two vocations, natural and supernatural, into one: we are at once in the world and beyond it, just as He, Jesus, is both here and beyond. We can fulfill this twofold but single vocation because *He* fulfills it—and He is in us.

Now Our Lord, through the successors of His Apostles, has told us what this vocation of ours must mean in a more particular way in these our times. We must help in the one great apostolate of the whole Church: to proclaim His Gospel where it has not yet been heard, and to give to those who have heard its proclamation a further instruction in its truth. Or, to use the imagery of St. Paul, we are to help "sow" the "seed" and "water" it (1 Cor 3:6). The "sowing" we call *evangelization*, and the "watering" we call *catechesis*.

But as we do these two things, we must remember that this seed which we sow and water—this Word of God which we proclaim and explain—will actually grow in the minds and souls of our hearers only by the grace of God. Only God can give the increase. And this should remind us, too, that what is true for the hearer is likewise true for the speaker. For how can we sow and cultivate the seed unless we already have it sown and cultivated in ourselves?

This brings us to the heart of our vocation, to the very core of our lives as followers and apostles of Jesus. We must *live* the truth before we can hope to proclaim and explain it as it was meant to be proclaimed and explained. For this seed is the living Word come down from Heaven and growing *in* the world by a power from *outside* the world (cf. Lk 8:11). We first received this seed—this Word—in a manner at least similar to what we are now doing for others: we had to hear this same Word proclaimed and explained to ourselves, coming to us from others who preceded us, until we get back to the first Apostles themselves (cf. Rom 11:14–15).

What we received was the Word of God, at once manifested and hidden in the words of men (cf. 1 Cor 2:1–4; 1 Tim 1:13). These human words, by God's power, are sacred and true: the words of the Creed and the Commandments, and the answering words of our prayers. These words taken together constitute our Gospel and our catechism; they comprise what we call the Faith. And we hold these words, this Faith, as received from those before us and as to be given to those following us, as our dearest treasure—dearer even than life itself.

This dearest treasure is indeed the Faith, for by it alone do we have contact with the Life which is eternal: the Life of the Triune God. Without it, therefore, we are hopelessly, eternally dead (cf. Heb 11:6). Yet, please note a most important distinction here, one which is essential to our proper understanding of the Faith and therefore to our proper *living* of it. That distinction is, precisely, that we can *have* this Faith in some sense without at the same time *living* it. Of course, all of us have always known of this distinction: mortal sin necessarily kills grace or charity, but it does not necessarily kill faith (Denzinger, no. 1578).

We may indeed believe all and only what the Church believes and teaches—in other words, we may be perfectly orthodox—but in and of itself we are not thereby saved. "Faith without good works is dead," St. James reminds us (Jas 2:26), and St. Paul himself says the same thing when he speaks of "faith working through love" (Gal 5:6). Indeed, so absolutely necessary is charity to the true "livingness" of faith that, as St. John tells us, if we do not *love* God we cannot really *know* Him—since God is love (1 Jn 4:8).

Faith leads to love, yes. But the reverse is also true: love leads to faith. As Our Lord Himself once told His enemies,

"He who is of God hears the words of God; the reason why you do not hear them is that you are not of God" (Jn 8:47).

These words of God, let us say it once more, are the human words of His Gospel: the Creed and the Commandments and the prayers that we call collectively "the Faith." This Faith may indeed—must indeed—be held by us as a treasure. But we must not make it a buried treasure! We may be inclined to treat it thus because of its very preciousness. The very expression, "Deposit of Faith," may perhaps induce this inclination on our part. And of all the faithful, we Catholics working to bring others into the Church may perhaps all too easily see our role as being just that: we are the champions of orthodoxy, the "keepers of the Faith"—and we may be "keeping" it by burying it—against that day when we must give an account of it.

But is this the right way to "keep the Faith"? We must not forget the Parable of the Talents (cf. Mt 25:14–30; Lk 19:12–28). Giving back to God the exact amount which He gave us—i.e., without interest or increase—will earn for us not His praise but His condemnation! No, the Faith is not some lump—some inert list of words, however sacred and true. Rather, the Faith is a seed: something therefore meant to grow—even if, yes, even if it thereby seems to die! We must never forget that in and of themselves the human words we speak of are not the Faith. They are but the signs—like the bread and wine of the Eucharist—of the one Reality of both faith and sacrament—the Reality which is the One Word of God, the Person Himself of Our Lord Jesus Christ.

LIVING IN THE WORLD YET NOT OF IT

Now, you may say, there is in what I have just now said a real hazard—and a real presumption. Is it not, indeed, a risk thus to expose the treasure of our Faith—the orthodoxy of our Fathers—to the hazards of this world? Do we not thus hazard the loss of the Faith, or at least its contamination, its diminution, its subtle erosion?

Yes, it is hazardous. But if others who had preceded us had not taken that risk, how would we ourselves have ever known and received the Faith? No, faith in all its aspects — its acceptance, its growth, its transmission — involves a great risk indeed. But did not Our Lord Himself assume a risk when He came down from Heaven to be with us — the risk of being for the fall as well as for the resurrection of many in Israel (cf. Lk 2:34)?

And as for the presumption implied here, we must admit that, so it seems. It does seem presumptuous of us thus to commit the Providence of God to our ventures, to count on Him to raise to life the dying seed of our Faith, to give increase to the seed we have sown and watered by our feeble efforts. Do we not have His Word for this? Is not the content of our Faith that very Word itself? And is not that Word deep within us — in our minds, in our hearts, in the deepest wellspring of our soul? Is not this therefore the only *real* orthodoxy — the Faith which is a total giving of ourselves to the God Who first gave Himself to us?

Yes, there is a risk here, a risk of over-simplification and audacity. But who is really more simple and audacious than Himself! — this Good Shepherd, this Jesus Who loves us to the end (cf. Jn 13:1)! Because He first has loved us (1 Jn 4:19), He now invites us — indeed, He commands us, He *dares* us! — to match Him love for love (cf. Jn 15:12–13)!

To such an invitation — to such a command and such a daring — what better response can we make than this response blessed by grace and Holy Church, this response of Catholics truly working to bring others to the Faith? Living in the world yet not of it, hearing the Word of God and pondering it in our hearts, our vocation is indeed "the better part" (Lk 10:42)!

With the original Apostles and their official successors, we dare not put ourselves (Acts 5:13). Rather, we put ourselves where God has put us: hidden and lowly in the midst of His people, His little ones — like the great saints we honor. Look at just one of our saints, Catherine of Siena, for example. Great precisely for her lowliness, she spoke before kings and pontiffs only because she had first spoken before God in her heart — and in that inner chamber heard His Word.

We put ourselves, then, with Catherine and all the blessed saints who with her have *decreased*, so that He the Bridegroom might *increase* (cf. Jn 3:30). But first and last, we put ourselves with her who alone fulfilled to absolute perfection this same vocation of ours. Blessed Mary Immaculate was also bid simply to hear the Word of God and keep it (Lk 11:28)—not as a buried talent but as a living seed! And if we now hear and keep that Word as she has, we too will bring forth in the world what has come from beyond it: the Eternal Word, Jesus Christ, the Son of the Living God.

As we continue to receive abundant grace, let us turn to the Triune God—through Christ Jesus, Who will renew among us and in us His Mystery of Faith. Let us thank Him for having given us His words in the Gospels in a manner even better than when He first gave them to His Apostles. For now we hear them on this side in time of His Passion and in the *pleroma* of His Paschal glory. He has proved, therefore, that the Seed having died does indeed bring forth fruit (Jn 12:24)!

And if we shall dare to bear Him after the manner of His Mother, we shall do so only because He has first borne us—His branches, His witnesses, His little ones—upon His shoulders and close to His beating Heart.

REFLECTIONS OF THE SAINTS

"Our only desire and our one choice should be this: I want and I choose what leads to God's deepening life in me.... He who goes about to reform the world must begin with himself, or he loses his labor." —ST. IGNATIUS OF LOYOLA

"An excellent method of preserving interior silence is to keep exterior silence.... [E]ven in the world, each one of us can make his own solitude, a boundary beyond which nothing can force its way unperceived. It is not noise in itself that is the difficulty, but noise that is pointless; it is not every conversation, but useless conversations; not all kinds of occupation, but aimless occupations. In point of fact, everything that does not serve some good purpose is harmful. It is foolish, nay, more, it is a betrayal to devote to a useless objective powers that can be given to what is essential. There are two ways of separating ourselves from Almighty God, quite different from one another but both disastrous, although for different reasons: mortal sin and voluntary distractions—mortal sin, which objectively breaks off our union with God, and voluntary distractions, which subjectively interrupt or hinder our union from being as close as it ought to be. We should speak only when it is preferable not to keep silence. The Gospel does not say merely that we shall have to give an account of every evil word, but of every idle thought." —ST. ALPHONSUS LIGUORI

"He will provide the way and the means, such as you could never have imagined. Leave it all to Him, let go of yourself, lose yourself on the Cross, and you will find yourself entirely." —ST. CATHERINE OF SIENA

"Only he will receive, will find, and will enter who perseveres in asking, seeking, and knocking. It is not enough to ask Almighty God for certain graces for a month, a year, ten, or even twenty years; we must never tire of asking. We must keep on asking until the very moment of death, and even in this prayer that shows our trust in God, we must join the thought of death to that of perseverance and say, 'Although He should kill me, I will trust in Him' (Job 13:15) and will trust Him to give me all I need." —ST. LOUIS-MARIE DE MONTFORT

"Jesus in the Blessed Sacrament is the most tender of friends with souls who seek to please Him. His goodness knows how to proportion itself to the smallest of His creatures as to the greatest of them. Be not afraid then in your solitary conversations, to tell Him of your miseries, fears, worries, of those who are dear to you, of your projects, and of your hopes. Do so with confidence and with an open heart." —ST. DAMIEN OF MOLOKAI

"He who enters into the secret place of his own soul passes beyond himself, and does in very truth ascend to God. Banish, therefore, from thy heart the distractions of earth and turn thine eyes to spiritual joys, that thou mayest learn at last to repose in the light of the contemplation of God." —ST. ALBERT THE GREAT

CHAPTER SEVEN

PENANCE: LEADING TO LIFE IN THE SACRED HEART

"You are Peter, and on this rock I will build my Church. And the gates of the underworld can never hold out against it. I will give you the keys of the kingdom of Heaven: whatever you bind on earth shall be considered bound in Heaven; whatever you loose on earth shall be considered loosed in Heaven" (Mt 16:18–20).

AS WE CONTINUE ON OUR JOURNEY TO live within the Sacred Heart of Jesus, it is certainly significant for us to consider the Sacrament of Penance. Any questioning of the importance of this sacrament in the context of the present critical time we live in would itself be one of the most obvious signs of the Church in crisis.

Significant too is the position assigned this chapter in our journey to the Sacred Heart. It has been put after the chapters on the Holy Eucharist as a kind of "last word." You might suggest that it would be more appropriate to discuss Penance toward the beginning, as with the Confiteor in the Mass, to get the penitential part over with first so that we could then get into the better and more positive things. But having it here after the Holy Eucharist is, I think, quite providential.

Why? *It reminds us that penance is never finished in this life.* Only with death (if indeed, even then!) is the "purgative way" of the spiritual life really completed. To think otherwise is the best proof that we have need of it! If we are to have an authentic renewal then, in our lives and in the Church and in the world at large, we must have penance—and Penance as sacramentalized by Christ—as an integral part of that renewal.

There is a clear Trinitarian pattern in our journey to the Sacred Heart of Jesus. We have moved from God the Father at the beginning, sending His only begotten Son into the world to redeem mankind, through God the Son and His mysteries of redemption, to God the Holy Spirit, the "Lord and Giver of Life."

Now finally we look to Him again, not so much as giving us remission of our sins as *being* that very remission itself—as that beautiful post-Communion prayer in the Traditional Latin Mass Pentecost Tuesday Octave put it:

> May the Holy Spirit, we beseech Thee, O Lord, renew our minds with the divine sacrament, for He is the remission of all sins. Through Our Lord Jesus Christ, Thy Son, Who lives and reigns with Thee, in the unity of the Holy Spirit, God forever and ever.

Here indeed we have the culmination of the Creed: "the forgiveness of sin" with its immediate correlative, "and life everlasting." Amen!

It is appropriate that we reflect upon two questions—First Confession and frequent confessions thereafter—especially in the context of the crisis in our times.

It may at first seem surprising that the Church's most comprehensive and solemn statement regarding the present crisis in the world, namely the Second Vatican Council, should mention the Sacrament of Penance so briefly and so few times—only nine times in all: once in the Constitution on the Church, once in the Constitution on the Liturgy, twice in the Decree on Bishops, and five times in the Decree on the Priestly Ministry. Of all the sacraments—with the possible exception of Extreme Unction, which the Council gave a new name, the Sacrament of the Sick—Penance is treated the least.

For all their paucity, however, these Conciliar references are richly pastoral. The intent of the Council Fathers to renew the use of this sacrament in the daily life of the Church is abundantly clear. We can see this in two typical passages. In the Dogmatic Constitution on the Church, we are told that

> [t]hose who approach the Sacrament of Penance obtain pardon from the mercy of God for offences committed against Him. They are at the same time reconciled with the Church, which they have wounded by their sins, and which by charity, example, and prayer seeks their conversion. (*Lumen gentium*, no. 11)

And again, in the Decree on the Priestly Ministry:

> In the spirit of Christ the Shepherd, priests should train the faithful to submit their sins with a contrite heart to the Church in the Sacrament of Penance. Thus, mindful of the Lord's words, 'Repent, for the kingdom of God is at hand,' the people will be drawn ever closer to Him every day. (*Presbyterorum ordinis*, no. 5)

But the best reason why the Council had so little to say about this Sacrament is that it had really little need to do so. All had been said, and quite adequately before. And the Council, as we shall see, quite clearly assumes this. Of all the previous moments in the history of the Magisterium, the most overwhelmingly monumental for the Sacrament of Penance, as also indeed for the Sacrament of the Holy Eucharist—the parallel here is most significant—is the Council of Trent. That great Council, as in so many other doctrinal matters, culminated a long development in the Church's ever deepening understanding of the immutable truth of her faith regarding this sacrament of Christ. In its Fourteenth Session (October–November 1551), the Council hammered out the nine chapters of its Decree on Penance, and summarized its doctrine in fifteen canons (cf. Denzinger, nos. 1667–93, 1701–15). What a formidable battery those canons were—the doom of heretics, both then and ever since!

THE ESSENTIAL TRIDENTINE DOCTRINE

It isn't necessary to recite all fifteen canons with their ringing anathemas, since the essential Tridentine doctrine can be summarized under two main points—two points which in turn summarized the entire previous history of the Church's understanding of her faith in Christ's instituting words. These two points are: (1) the *power of absolution* as the absolute forgiveness of all sins committed and repented of by baptized Christians, as mediated by the Church through her authorized minister acting in the name of Christ; and (2) the *necessity of confession* as the integral act of the penitent, preceded by contrition and followed by satisfaction, submitting his sins to the judgment of the Church through her same authorized minister acting in the name of Christ. These two points thus summarize a mutual totality of commitment meeting in the person-to-person confrontation of penitent and priest: the baptized sinner's total commitment to repent and God's total commitment to forgive.

To the comprehensiveness and clarity of these irreformable Tridentine definitions thus summarized, we owe, in God's providence, the strength and "style" of the modern Church. No wonder that the subsequent Magisterium up to and including the Second Vatican Council had relatively so little to say on the matters treated at Trent.

However, it would be a mistake to suppose that the Church has been any less active after Trent than she was before in her constant reflection upon the content of her Faith. There had always been, and there will always be, this "development of doctrine," this ever greater explicitation of the germinal, immutable truths as revealed by Christ.

In the case of the Sacrament of Penance this development followed in perfect continuity the Tridentine development itself: the mutually related necessity and efficacy of the Sacrament were further delineated. The two fundamental facts—the fact of *sin* and the fact of *forgiveness*—were more clearly seen as co-extensive with the total life of the Christian.

"Sin" meant *all* sin, even the so-called venial sins, the sins that need not be submitted to the Sacrament for forgiveness since they do not actually kill the life of grace. But they are sins nonetheless. They impede the life of grace, just as in turn that life of grace makes more evident their reality of evil.

Likewise, "forgiveness" took on deeper meaning. It meant no longer a kind of minimal thing: the restoration of grace just sufficient for salvation. Rather, it meant something dynamic and infinitely open to growth—a fountain of water springing up into life everlasting!

Concretely, this deepening awareness of the Church's Faith found expression in a small but most significant succession of statements by the Magisterium. The following three instances suffice. In 1794 Pope Pius VI condemned as

> 'temerarious, pernicious and contrary to the practice of saints and holy persons as approved by the Council of Trent' the declaration of the Jansenist Synod of Pistoia that the confession of venial sins should not become so frequent as to expose such confessions to contempt. (Denzinger, no. 2639)

In other words, the Church would assume the same risk as Christ had assumed: the *possibility of abuse* would be accepted, if only the *efficacy of use* were increased!

This same doctrine, confirmed through subsequent generations by the ordinary Magisterium and the practice of the Church, was explicitly reiterated and amplified in 1945 when Pope Pius XII thus spoke in his great encyclical on the Mystical Body of Christ:

> Not the spiritual advancement of the faithful but their tragic ruin would follow from the opinions of those who assert that little importance should be given to the frequent confession of venial sins. Of far greater importance, they say, is that general confession which the Spouse of Christ surrounded by her children in the Lord makes each day by the mouth of the priest as he approaches the altar. It is true indeed, Venerable Brothers, that venial sins may be expiated in many ways which are to be highly commended. But to hasten daily progress along the path of virtue We wish the pious practice of frequent confession to be earnestly advocated. Not without the inspiration of the Holy Spirit was this practice introduced into the Church. By it genuine self-knowledge is increased, Christian humility grows, bad habits are corrected, spiritual neglect and tepidity are countered, the conscience is purified, the

> will strengthened, a salutary self-control is attained, and grace is increased in virtue of the sacrament itself. Let those, therefore, among the young clergy who make light of or weaken esteem of frequent confession realize that what they are doing is foreign to the Spirit of Christ, and disastrous for the Mystical Body of our Savior. (*Mystici Corporis*, no. 95; cf. Denzinger, no. 3818)

Finally, let me cite a statement which actually preceded this last-mentioned one, but which emphasizes only one aspect of this topic of frequent confession, namely, the all-important aspect of *when* in the life of the Christian this practice should begin. In 1910 St. Pius X decreed that "from [the age of the use of reason] there begins the obligation to satisfy the precept concerning annual confession and communion" (*Quam singulari*, no. 1; cf. Denzinger, no. 3530). He further decreed that "the custom of not admitting children to confession or of not absolving them, although they have reached the use of reason, is by no means to be allowed" (*Quam singulari*, no. 7; cf. Denzinger, no. 3536).

In all three instances the connection between the two sacraments, of Penance and the Holy Eucharist, is evident. The frequent reception of these two sacraments is, we can safely say, the most authentic and efficacious sign of the integral Christian life. And if this was always so implicitly in past ages, it is explicitly so in our present time.

The Magisterium for our present time is, of course, primarily the Second Vatican Council. And, as we have said, the very paucity of its references to the Sacrament of Penance argues to its simple assumption of the continuity and adequacy of the preceding Tradition.

But there is now more to be said. Unquestionably the most distinctive and consequential statement of the Council concerning Penance is the following brief directive in the Constitution on the Liturgy:

> The rite and formulas for the Sacrament of Penance are to be revised, so that they give more luminous expression to both the nature and the effect of the sacrament. (*Sacrosanctum Concilium*, no. 72)

In this one short sentence the Council commits the Church to a "revision"—but not without clearly stating *what* is to be revised, and *why*. In view of so many other misunderstandings of the Council's intentions that have occurred, it is important that we here understand very clearly both the object and the reason of the required revision concerning this Sacrament.

The object, first of all, is quite clear: "the rite and formulas," the external ceremonies surrounding the essential sacramental act. The distinction here, as in all the sacraments, between what is of Christ and therefore immutable, and what is of the Church and therefore mutable, is axiomatic. In fact, of all the sacraments, Penance has had perhaps the greatest variations over the centuries in its "rite and formulas." The possibility of a further revision, therefore, is both historically and dogmatically certain.

But because a thing is possible it by no means follows that it is desirable. The desirability of a revision must depend, then, on the second point of the Conciliar directive: the reason it specifies must be verified. And that one reason, necessary and sufficient, is that there should be a "more luminous expression to both the nature and effect of the sacrament." The immutable truth of the Sacrament—its nature and effect as instituted by Christ and defined previously by the Church—must now be made more evident, more luminous to our times.

SECULAR HUMANISM POISONING OUR CULTURE

To provide her children with some better understanding of this Sacrament of Penance is perhaps the most important single way by which the Church can meet—immediately and head-on—the crisis of our time.

For in what, after all, does this present crisis consist? And from what does it stem? It consists essentially in a mass movement of secular humanism that has for some centuries now dominated our western culture, and with it the world. And this secular humanism stems from a single fundamental source: *the doctrine of man's self-sufficiency, his independence from God.*

There have been historically two variant versions of this secular humanism. The first, coming out of the eighteenth century Enlightenment, was Rationalism: the deification of man and the inevitable perfection of the world that through science and benevolence he would create on this earth. In direct opposition to this optimism, the Church's defined doctrine of *the fact of sin* and the consequent necessity of confession was not only an affront—it was nonsense. The Church's strictness was simply inhuman; it could not be taken seriously.

But then, how seriously could Rationalism itself be taken? In the nineteenth-century reaction to the Enlightenment a second form of secular humanism came to dominate our culture. Succeeding the naïve optimism of the Rationalists, based on their deification of man, came the murky pessimism of the Romanticists, debasing man to the level of "nature"—a "naked ape," lost even to himself. Squarely facing this pessimism stood the Church's other defined doctrine of the fact of forgiveness and the consequent power of absolution. But again, the world would not have it. It was too lenient. The mere word of a priest could never reach the real "ego," buried as it was under so many layers of "id."

This brief analysis of the internal disintegration and bankruptcy of secular humanism as a consistent doctrine, and of its peculiarly paradoxical polarization in the face of the Catholic doctrine on penance, is no doubt interesting and helpful. But it must not distract us from the much more important point, namely, the *single* fundamental error from which both varieties have sprung. The differences between Rationalism and Romanticism, as also between formal Atheism and agnostic Liberalism, are superficial—even trivial—when compared with what they all have in common. For, as the great Dietrich von Hildebrand has reminded us, the truth does not stand between these various extremes, but above them. It differs from both positions much more than they differ from each other (cf. *Trojan Horse in the City of God*, ch. 3).

That one common error is what we have already stated it to be: the doctrine of man's self-sufficiency, of his independence from God. In diametric opposition stands the Catholic doctrine of man's creaturehood, of his absolute dependence on God. God made man to be man: he is neither a god nor a brute—he is free and responsible—*for better or for worse.*

Thus, the Church's two defined facts, of sin and of forgiveness, are really but two facets of the one defined fact of *repentance*. And thus, her position is neither too strict nor too lenient, and both "optimism" and "pessimism," as the world defines them, are to her irrelevant. Indeed, the world's attitude, for all its superficial variety, is fundamentally but one thing—an enormous *presumption*, a presumption to repeal reality. And as always happens with presumption, the only ultimate end is *despair*.

It might seem that in view of this terrible crisis of our time—stemming directly as it does from its rejection of the Catholic doctrine on sin (confession) and forgiveness (absolution) as defined at the Council of Trent—the best course of action, indeed the only course, would be simply to repeat that doctrine as clearly and patiently as we can, until the world in its despair will heed it at last. It is so desperately evident that Catholics must be convinced of the need for the Sacrament of Penance as a prelude to the Sacrament of the Holy Eucharist.

THE QUESTION OF REVISIONS

And indeed, that is precisely what the Second Vatican Council, as we have seen, meant by its "revision." That revision, after these several years now since the Council, in June 2021 achieved a completely definitive form in the United States when the U. S. Conference of Catholic Bishops voted to amend the Order of Penance as part of a broader effort to align liturgical texts more closely to the Latin version. The Latin version from the Vatican maintains in its structure individual confession and a communal aspect in which multiple penitents attend a service but confess individually. This form is used by many parishes during Advent and Lent. The new order of the Rite of Penance in the United States became effective on Ash Wednesday 2023. That it took so long to complete a Revised Order of Penance indicates the difficulty of the task!

Any revisions of the Sacrament of Penance going forward, whatever their variant forms, cannot *supplant* the existing discipline (namely, of private and integral confession, with absolution in a judicial form) without putting in grave question the immutability of the nature and effect of the Sacrament.

Before I proceed to my conclusion as to what any further revisions required by the Council really and ultimately must be, let me digress a moment on another and rather ominous aspect of this general question of revision and of some of the responses to it that have been made. Just as in the case of the Holy Eucharist—the parallel between the two Sacraments is always a most significant one—the invitation to revision has on balance raised more questions than it has solved! It has encouraged some critics of the present discipline to question whether *any* revision is really adequate. For there are now arising *doctrinal* questions going far beyond this or that *disciplinary* reform. Just as the changes affecting certain "rites and formulas" in the Mass have occasioned theories and experiments that the Council Fathers would never have imagined as seriously entertainable by professing Catholics, so too any additional changes affecting Penance are fraught with danger.

For the real question for some "Catholic" critics now is not whether confession should be private and integral or public and general, not whether absolution should be judicial or impetrative. Rather, it is whether there is any sense to *any* confession or to *any* absolution at all.

This "God-talk" in the sacraments, we are now being told, is but a hypothesis that the "new theology" is wondering how long it can continue to support! Which means, of course, that we are right back to the secular humanism which created the crisis in the first place. Only now, it is attacking the very basis of supernatural religion from within the Catholic Church.

From this rather gloomy assessment of the problems facing any future revisions of the rite and formulas of Penance, we may be tempted to conclude that we had better leave well enough alone! As the years have gone by since the Council ended, we have but to regret a Conciliar exuberance, which may have been justified regarding other sacraments, but not this one! To change the rite and formula of the Sacrament of Penance to be more compatible with modern times is a view I cannot share, for I maintain that we now have the opportunity—the obligation—to make "more luminous the expression" of this sacrament, seeing as how exactly it meets the crisis of our time.

What, then, could be such a revision as I have in mind? Simply and profoundly: It is one of *education.* The real problem, after all, is not what to tell the penitent who has already committed himself to the reception of the Sacrament. Rather, it is what to tell the baptized Christian to convince him he is a sinner and in need of forgiveness, so that he may with conscientiousness and gratitude commit himself to its reception.

This educative task is by nature prior to the properly sacramental one. And in this age of dimmed recognition of sin against God and of the urgency of His pardon, that task is only the more comprehensive and demanding. This very same educative approach to the desired revision is clearly intimated in those few but pointed pastoral directives that the Second Vatican Council addressed to both bishops and priests, and that we have already referred to. From their context it is clear that what is envisaged as the fitting matter of the Sacrament are *all* the sins of *all* the faithful.

In line with the great popes preceding it, the Council sees this Sacrament as the divinely provided and preeminent means not merely of reconciliation but of growth. It is not merely for the "great sinner" but for all the faithful, not merely for treating in an ad hoc fashion the symptoms of special sin but for eradicating from the Christian body the pervasive terrible evils of this critical time in the Twenty-First Century of the Church.

A BAPTISMAL RIGHT TO KNOW

If our main revisionary task, then, is one of education, and if education must always begin with the earliest years to be most effective, then we have before us—clearly and unmistakably—the unspoken mandate of the Council. The

Conciliar revisions to the Sacrament, wherever and however they may eventually end, must unequivocally begin with the instruction of Christ's newest members in the authentic doctrine of the Holy Church regarding the immutable truth of this Sacrament of Penance.

Children judged old enough to recognize the Body of Christ in the Holy Eucharist are also old enough to recognize offenses against that Body. Especially in this age of mass communication, when children are deliberately manipulated in the interests of a world proclaiming its self-sufficiency, we must see to it that their baptismal right to the knowledge of God and His truth is respected and secured. The stakes at issue are too high to permit delay. Here as nowhere else will be decided the question of whether and when the present crisis of our world will be finally resolved on the side of truth.

Although the Council's mandate on this matter is unspoken, the tradition of the Magisterium both preceding and following the Council most emphatically is not. The Sacred Congregation of the Clergy in 1971, with the full approval of Pope Paul VI, concluded its *General Catechetical Directory* with a special Addendum, "First Approach to the Sacraments of Penance and the Eucharist," which enjoins the following discipline on the Universal Church:

> All things considered, having in view the common and general practice, which cannot be modified without the approval of the Holy See, after consulting the Episcopal Conferences, the same Holy See judges it expedient that the now-flourishing custom of putting confession before first Communion should be preserved; this does not prevent the custom from being improved in various ways, as, for example, by a communal penitential celebration before or after the child approaches the Sacrament of Penance. (no. 5)

This statement of the Magisterium is in perfect harmony with all that we have learned over all the centuries of the Catholic doctrine on the Sacrament of Penance. Open to disciplinary revision within the framework of defined truth, we must be as the Church our Mother.

And let us not forget the responsibility that we as members of this household of the Faith must bear. For better or for worse, we are Catholics—the baptized Christians to whom has been confided this gift of God. How we use it is a responsibility that those who have no faith or baptism do not share. *Their sin* is indeed an offence against God, Father and Son, rejecting as they do the mysteries of Creation and Redemption. But *our sin* will be something more; it will be against the Holy Spirit. From Our Lord's own words, we know what *that* means, and so we take heed.

With these words of Christ and His Church resounding in our minds and challenging our wills, we may now conclude this disquisition with an appeal to our hearts, simple yet profound. If secular humanism, both outside and inside the Church, were to single out the symbol most radically inimical to its own view of the world and man, that symbol would unquestionably be the Sacred Heart of Jesus Christ, true God and true Man. For here is the Sign *par excellence* of the abounding of sin and the more abounding of pardon.

At once too strict and too lenient for the votaries of this world, the immutable truth of this Penitential Sacrament of Christ, hater of sin and lover of sinners, stands forever symbolized by His Sacred Heart. And well for us that it so stands, for here—amid this world's despair—shines the sole and all-sufficing *hope of our hearts.*

REFLECTIONS FROM THE SAINTS

"In the life of the body a man is sometimes sick, and unless he takes medicine, he will die. Even so in the spiritual life a man is sick on account of sin. For that reason, he needs medicine so that he may be restored to health; and this grace is bestowed in the Sacrament of Penance."—ST. THOMAS AQUINAS

"By Christ's Passion our weakness was cured. By His Resurrection death was conquered. Still, we have to be sorrowful for the world, as well as joyful in the Lord, sorrowful in penance, joyful in gratitude."—ST. AMBROSE OF MILAN

"See blind ones, deceived by your enemies, by the flesh, the world, and the devil; that it is sweet to the body to work sin and bitter to work to serve God. Because all vices and sins come forth and 'proceed from the heart of man,' just as the Lord says in the Gospel (cf. Mk 7:21). And you shall have nothing in this age nor to the one to come. And you think you will possess the vanities of this generation [*saeculum*] for a long time, but you have been deceived, since there shall come the day and hour, of which you do not think, know, or pay attention; the body weakens, death approaches, and thus one dies a bitter death. And wherever, whenever, a man dies in culpable sin, without penance and satisfaction, if he can make satisfaction and does not make satisfaction, the devil tears his soul from his body with such anguish and tribulation, that no one can know it, except him who experiences it." —ST. FRANCIS OF ASSISI

"Review then, in careful thought the innumerable blessings wherewith thy Creator has ennobled thee, no merits of thine own intervening; and call to mind thine own unnumbered evils thy sole response—O, how wicked and how undeserved!—for all those His benefits; and cry out in the pangs of a great grief, 'What have I done? Provoked my God, challenged my Creator's anger, repaid Him innumerable ills for untold goods. What have I done?' And speaking thus, rend, rend thy heart, pour forth sighs, weep showers of tears. For if thou weepest not here, when will thou weep?" —ST. ANSELM OF CANTERBURY

"If the poor world could see the beauty of the sinless soul, all sinners, all unbelievers would be instantly converted." —ST. PADRE PIO

"Behold, Jesus Christ crucified, Who is the only foundation of our hope; He is our mediator and advocate, the victim and sacrifice for our sins. He is goodness and patience itself; His mercy is moved by the tears of sinners, and He never refuses pardon and grace to those who ask it with a truly contrite and humbled heart." —ST. CHARLES BORROMEO

"Our soul is like a hot-air balloon. If by chance there is a mortal sin, the soul falls to the ground. Confession is like the fire underneath the balloon enabling the soul to rise again. It is important to go to confession often." —ST. CARLO ACUTIS

CHAPTER EIGHT

SALVIFICI DOLORIS: A REFLECTION ON SUFFERING

> *"Be calm, but vigilant, because your enemy the devil is prowling round like a roaring lion, looking for someone to eat. Stand up to him, strong in faith and in the knowledge that your brothers all over the world are suffering the same things. You will have to suffer only for a little while: the God of all grace who called you to eternal glory to Christ will see that all is well again. He will confirm, strengthen and support you. His power lasts forever and ever. Amen"* (1 Peter 5:8–11).

THE JOURNEY TO LIVE WITHIN THE SACRED Heart of Jesus will come with much suffering. It is not an easy journey as you will be participating in His suffering. St. Paul, who suffered much, interiorly and from the trials he underwent on his missionary journey, reminds us: "For the Lord trains the ones He loves and he punishes all those that he acknowledges as His sons. *Suffering is part of your training*; God is treating you as His sons" (Heb 12:6–7).

As Mother Angelica of the Poor Clares of Perpetual Adoration said in her book, *On Suffering and Burnout*, "*We cannot choose a cross.* We cannot decide what suffering is best for the training of our invisible souls. We must grow strong in a way known only to God, for few of us know ourselves or our weaknesses well enough to choose the suffering best suited to change us" (p. 10).

On February 11, 1984, during the Holy Year of Redemption, Pope St. John Paul II issued an apostolic letter, *Salvifici doloris*, exploring the Christian meaning of suffering. His objective was to show the connection between our suffering as humans and Christ's redemptive suffering on the Cross.

In this letter, His Holiness reminded us that suffering is a universal experience; no one is exempt from it during their lives as it is an integral part of human existence. As such, suffering can have a profound meaning and purpose for us within the context of our Catholic Faith.

He then highlighted the concept of "salvific suffering," which can lead us to spiritual growth and our own redemption. Drawing upon the teachings of St. Paul, who spoke of completing what was lacking in Christ's afflictions for the sake of the Church, Pope John Paul urged all of us to look upon suffering as our participation in Christ's own suffering. By doing this, we are on the path to our own salvation.

Linking our suffering to the virtues of hope and love, the letter emphasized that through suffering we can grow in compassion with others, which helps us foster a deeper connection to our neighbors, the greater community, and God. Through our personal suffering, we can draw closer to Jesus and thus to one another. His Holiness advised us not to look upon suffering through a lens of despair but instead to embrace it and recognize it as a pathway that leads us to a greater love of Jesus and brings us to dwell within His Sacred Heart.

The Holy Father reminded us that suffering, being "inseparable from man's earthly existence," is most appropriately "the way for the Church." It seems fitting that we project, as it were, the Holy Year of Redemption into and through the rest of our lives by a brief summary of this meditation. Just as the solemnity of the Sacred Heart completes and perfects the liturgical cycle by linking the Paschal season with the rest of the year, so may we offer this modest essay as a postscript, a complement, to the Papal teaching on salvific suffering.

A LIFE OF PERFECTION ITSELF

The high point of St. John's Gospel (which in turn is the high point of the New Testament) is the ultimate and supreme revelation: Christ's opened Heart on the Cross. Its ultimateness is indicated by the last word spoken by the dying Jesus as recorded by the same Evangelist: "It is finished" (Jn 19:30). In the total Johannine context that one little word, *tetelestai* (in the Vulgate: *consummatum est*), summarized perfectly the earthly mortal life of Jesus Christ.

That life was perfection itself—in its entirety and in all its parts, even to the smallest detail; it was that drop of vinegar and its attendant fulfillment of prophecy which occasioned this last word. It was literally and absolutely perfect, as planned from eternity by God His Father. His Father's will: here was the one determinant, the one cause, the one explanation of everything for Jesus (see Jn 4:34; 5:30; 8:29; 12:49–50; 14:10). His mission in time was, as it were, an extension of His procession from eternity—He comes forth from the Father, and to the Father He returns (Jn 16:28).

This "circuitry"—which *is* the Holy Spirit—is perfect in its unity and wholeness. Nothing can undo it, impede it, or in any way modify it. This is the reason for that serene independence, that majestic freedom, that absolute "indifference" (in the Ignatian sense) which characterizes Our Lord's every word and gesture, as recorded by all the Evangelists and especially St. John.

It was His first word, spoken in the womb of His mother: "a body hast thou prepared for me.... Then I said, 'Behold, I come to do thy will, O God'" (Heb 10:5, 7). It is His last word, spoken on the night before He died: "Father, I have finished the work thou gavest me to do... and now I come to Thee." (Jn 17:4, 13). "*Tetelestai—consummatum est*—it is finished."

The truth of Christ's sovereign activity, even in—especially in—His Passion, is thus evident: "No one takes my life from me; I lay it down of myself" (Jn 10:18). However, there is a second and complementary truth equally evident. In coming into the world, the Eternal Word accepted to the full the limitations of the complete created nature He assumed. As a creature His existence and even His decisions were affected by the existence and decisions of other creatures. The very body prepared for Him came as a direct result of another's free consent: His Mother's "fiat" (Lk 1:38). His place of birth was decided by Caesar Augustus.

Where—and indeed even whether—He could exercise His ministry of miracles and preaching was decided by others: His fellow Nazarenes (Mk 6:5), the Gadarene strangers across the lake (Mt 8:34), the officialdom of Judea (Jn 7:1). And finally and supremely His Passion. The very word "Passion" says it—it was not so much what He *did* as what *was done* to Him. Judas, Caiphas, Pilate—they all had decisions to make regarding Jesus, and they made their decisions freely (Mt 26:24; Jn 11:49–50; Jn 19:11). Theirs was the giving end, the action. The receiving end, the Passion, was Christ's. Even the ultimate revelation of His Sacred Heart was "passive," dependent as it was on the action of another, the centurion's thrust of the lance.

These two truths in combination form a paradox, which of course should not surprise us. The entire Gospel, indeed the whole of revelation, is but one great paradox: the paradox of real beings distinct from the one Being—more specifically, of creaturely freedom in the face of divine omnipotence; and most specifically of all, of real sin co-existing with infinite love. These two truths are complementary. They are meant to be combined in the integral oneness of the truth as revealed. Note the complete fusion of the two truths in this one sentence—a key sentence—in the first Christian sermon, St. Peter's Pentecost *kerygma*: "This Jesus, delivered up according to the definite plan and foreknowledge of God, you crucified and killed by the hands of lawless men" (Acts 2:23).

Thus, suffering was no mere "accident" in Christ's earthly life. There were, in the deepest sense, no "might-have-beens" with Him. His life was not cut short or diverted or in any way curtailed by the decisions of men. Rather, it was fulfilled to perfection; it was "consummated"—finished—not in spite of but because of what He suffered. Such is the infinite wisdom and power at the service of the Providence that is love. "Although He was a Son, He learned obedience through what He suffered; and being made perfect He became the source of eternal salvation to all who obey Him" (Heb 5:8–9).

WHAT ABOUT OURSELVES?

Turning now to ourselves, we can see in the light of Christ Crucified (and only in the light) the meaning of our existence, and its inseparable constituent: suffering. First of all, we see, as the Holy Father remarks early on in his letter, that suffering—human suffering—cannot be defined apart from moral evil: sin. In the vocabulary of the Old Testament, suffering and evil are identified with each other. With no special Scriptural word for "suffering," the true dimensions of evil—moral evil—become, in the consciousness of the Scriptures, all-embracing. Not the so-called "ontic evil" of modern philosophers, the mere fact of contingency and limitation in the creature, but rather the privation of a creaturely good, a privation in some way referable to man—to his dignity and freedom.

Thus, even such purely physical causes of pain as earthquakes, storms, or wild beasts are attributable in some way to how man, the lord of creation, has borne himself in his unique relationship to his Lord, the Creator God (see Rom 8:21–22). It was this ever broadening and deepening concept of *sin* as responsible for *all* suffering that gives the Book of Job its power and poignancy.

Yet, as we know from the New Testament, Job's conscience and cry are vindicated, but not without a yet deeper mystery. There is certainly a connection between suffering and sin; but, as Our Lord made clear in the case of the man born blind, that connection is not always easy to determine (Jn 9:3).

And in His own case, once more, what can we say? The Passion of Christ was at once the unjust suffering of perfect innocence and the just suffering of Him Whom St. Paul dares to call "sin" itself (2 Cor 5:21).

Applying now the same paradox to ourselves, can we not say that here precisely is the one essential factor of all suffering as such? It may be but the least displeasure or it may be the most crushing pain. But what causes it to be *suffering* is simply and exclusively the fact that we must "take it." There is no action, no "control," on our part; we *cannot understand* it.

In our purely subjective experience, which is the greater suffering: to suffer because we know we deserve it (e.g., the humiliation brought about by our deceitfulness exposed, the accident caused by our willful negligence, the illness caused by our over-indulgence)? Or to suffer because we know we do not deserve it (e.g., the humiliation brought about by a mistaken identity, the accident in which we were simply a bystander, the illness that we in no way foresaw or could have foreseen)? The very fact that in each of these instances we instinctively feel that we would suffer *less* if the cause of the suffering were *other* than what we think it is, is perhaps the clearest sign of this very essence of suffering: we cannot understand it, we cannot control it, we simply must take it.

When, moreover, this paradox is cast in *time*—as, being human, it must be—this essence of suffering is "completed" by our feeling that henceforth our personality is, to whatever degree, curtailed, left unfinished, deprived of the full actuality it was capable of. Nothing brings us closer to the heart of suffering than our dwelling on what *might have been.*

And yet there is, in this same context of time, the further paradox in this mystery of misery and mercy that is suffering. Suffering itself can be a "might-have-been." Which was the better thing: pride in our humiliation, or humility? Should there have been pleasure in our pain, or only pain? Can we go on failing in our failure, and find worth in it? Yes! Such is our misery and God's mercy that our suffering needs but a *moment* of time—a moment at the last—for *all* to be made good, for *all* to be finally completed. See the dying Good Thief on the cross!

THERE STANDS CHRIST THE CRUCIFIED

The human suffering thus described is common to all and unique to each. And its connection with sin becomes all the more deeply mysterious when we remember that the one person who suffered the most—in part at least because of not being able to "understand" (Lk 2:50)—was Mary Immaculate. The rest of us, from the great saints down, are sinners—sinners both in our common nature and in our proper persons. Thus, suffering is at once the most common and the most unique reality: that to which and in which we can all relate, and that in which and because of which we are utterly alone.

Now, facing all this humanity in its universality and in each of its individuals, as the Holy Father vividly portrays Him, stands Christ the Crucified. As a divine Person, He understands all reality with infinite perfection. And even in His human consciousness, all the treasures of wisdom and knowledge are His (Col 2:3). His suffering is absolutely *exclusive*, for He alone sees God. (The Beatific Vision, far from rendering Him immune to suffering, makes it so immeasurably more real that in comparison with it, all other suffering is but its faintest analogue.)

Yet at the same time His suffering is absolutely *inclusive*, for He alone is Everyman, the New Adam, the Redeemer. Only in connection with Him does all human suffering become intelligible.

This means that there must be some reciprocal exchange between Our Lord and ourselves. His suffering calls for cure, for He cannot suffer as we do unless we allow Him to suffer in us. And our sufferings call for His, for we cannot understand our sufferings unless we suffer in Him—to which suffering, with the insistence of merciful love, He invites us (Mt 11:28–30; Jn 14:4). He takes our misery in His mercy, and the two are fused into the one Suffering that is the redemption of the world.

Only by this mutual "abiding" will there be the perfection, the completion, the "finish" willed by the Father: our making up what is wanting in the suffering of Christ (Col 1:24) and Christ perfecting the infirmity which is ourselves (2 Cor 12:9).

S*alvifici doloris*: this mutual suffering is essentially salvific. Not by His preaching and miracles—not by His "action"—did Christ save the world, but by His Passion. His actions were important, but they were only dispositive, preparing for the completion of Redemption that came only on the Cross.

Likewise, our cooperation with the Redemption consists essentially, not in our "action" but in our "passion." Christ's words and deeds are all quite complete already — as complete as the Deposit of Faith contains them. But, as we have seen, there is an "incompleteness" in His sufferings, which only we can make good. Our actions have their role and their efficacy; but ultimately and inevitably they lead — as they are meant to lead, by God's "definite plan and foreknowledge" — to suffering. Indeed, this is "the way" for the Church and for us.

The Father wills to place us with His Son; and so, with the same "indifference" that Jesus had in His earthly life, we follow Him into the surrender, the abandonment, that He had in death. For only thus upon His Cross, and within His very Heart now opened for us to enter, can we complete our lives.

Our seeming abandonment by God and our actual abandonment to Him — this is the single finishing perfection of the "total Christ" — to be hidden now until the Resurrection, but to be proclaimed in glorious anticipation by that one word now made our own: "*Tetelestai — consummatum est* — it is finished."

But as we live and wake up in the world each day, suffering comes to us, and it comes to us every day, whether with heavy crosses or light ones made of balsa wood. To help us carry our crosses and be sustained on our journey, St. Ignatius of Loyola has given us a beautiful and encouraging prayer, the *Anima Christi*, which appears at the beginning of the *Spiritual Exercises*:

Soul of Christ, sanctify me.
Body of Christ, save me.
Blood of Christ, inebriate me.
Passion of Christ, strengthen me.
O good Jesus, hear me.
Within Thy wounds hide me.
Suffer me not to be separated from Thee.
From the malignant enemy, defend me.
In the hour of my death, call me.
And bid me come to Thee.
That with Thy saints I may praise Thee.
Forever and ever. Amen.

MEDITATIONS FROM THE SAINTS

"Sufferings are the wings with which I take my flight to Heaven." —ST. CYPRIAN

"You have to love while you are suffering and suffer while you are loving." —ST. JOHN VIANNEY

"If God causes you to suffer much, it is a sign that He has great designs for you. There is no wood better to kindle the fire of holy love than the wood of the Cross." —ST. IGNATIUS OF LOYOLA

"He will never let the trial surpass the strength He gives you, and at the very moment you think yourself overwhelmed by sorrow, He will lift you up and give you peace." —ST. ROSE PHILIPPINE DUCHESNE

"O Lord, Jesus Christ, two favors I beg of you before I die. The first is that I may, as far as it is possible, feel in my soul and in my body the suffering in which you, O gentle Jesus, sustained in your bitter Passion. And the second favor is that I, as far as it is possible, may receive in my heart that excessive charity by which you, the Son of God, were inflamed, and which actuated you willingly to suffer so much for us sinners." —ST. FRANCIS OF ASSISI

"The reason why the soul not only travels securely when in obscurity, but also makes greater progress, is this: In general the soul makes greater progress in the spiritual life when it least thinks so, yea, when it rather imagines that it is losing everything.... There is another reason also why the soul has traveled safely in this obscurity; it has suffered: for the way of suffering is safer, and also more profitable than that of rejoicing and of action. In suffering God gives strength, but in action and in joy the soul does but show its own weakness and imperfections. And in suffering, the soul practices and acquires virtue, and becomes pure, wiser, and more cautious." —ST. JOHN OF THE CROSS

"You will be consoled according to the greatness of your sorrow and affliction; the greater the suffering, the greater will be the reward." —ST. MARY MAGDALEN DE' PAZZI

"When I shrink from suffering, Jesus reproves me and tells me that He did not refuse to suffer. Then I say 'Jesus, your will be done and not mine.'" —ST. GEMMA GALGANI

CHAPTER NINE

THE MOST SACRED HEART OF JESUS

"When they came to Jesus, they found He was already dead, and so instead of breaking His legs, one of the soldiers pierced His side with a lance; and immediately there came out blood and water" (Jn 19:33–35).

IF IT CAN BE SAID, AS A GREAT WRITER ONCE put it, that a period of history can be the best of times and the worst of times, then such a period of history is right now. Whether in terms of opportunity or in terms of peril, there has never been a time quite like our own. This is what we mean by crisis, and even the fact that the word has become overworked and we have become numbed to these constant calls of crisis, as we see the situation as more critical, we must in our turn be more critical. We must judge of the judgment that is impending.

We must take to heart as Pope St. John XXIII did when he called the Vatican Council and gave it a task—and a task for us all—to take to *our* hearts the signs of the times.

Now of all the signs of the times, of all the things that symbolize the realities of our condition—a hand with a hammer, a finger on a button, a footprint on the moon, the face of a fetus in the womb—of all these signs, there is one surely that is the deepest and truest and most critical of all. That sign is the *human heart*.

Let me quote an unforgettable passage from the Vatican Council's great document on the Church and our time, *Gaudium et spes*, in the section on "the Essential Nature of Man":

> Man is not deceived when he regards himself as superior to bodily concerns and as more than just a speck of nature or a nameless constituent of the city of man. For by his interior qualities—his interiority—he outstrips the whole sum of mere things. He finds reinforcement in this profound insight whenever he enters into his own heart. God who probes the heart awaits him there, and where he himself decides his own destiny in the sight of God. So, when he recognizes in himself a spiritual and immortal soul, he is not being led astray by false imaginings that are due to merely physical or social causes. On the contrary, he grasps what is profoundly truth in this matter.

The human heart, this physical organ in the center of the body, is the natural sign of the center of the whole person, his innermost self, his feelings, his understandings, his questions, his unfathomable desires. Every language uses this same symbol. To all mankind and to all ages, the heart means the same one thing.

We have said with the Council that God who probes the heart awaits man there. What if we were to say that the converse is equally true, that man can find God by finding that *He too has a heart*, that God, the ground of our being, the judge of our judgments, the source and goal of our destiny, has in His turn an inner-most self residing in a physical organ centered in a human body.

To say such a thing is literally true. And this literal truth has been said now for 2,000 years, that God, in the person of His Incarnate Son, Jesus Christ, has a heart and that heart has been revealed to us to make certain that we do not mistake it or think it too good to be true. This is the public and final climax of that definitive revelation we call the New Testament.

I refer therefore not just to private revelations, those shared secrets of the saints, and especially of St. Margaret Mary Alacoque, that we properly hold in total belief and veneration. I am referring rather to Scripture itself. And just as the entire written Gospel has its high point obviously in the soaring Gospel of St. John, so his Gospel has its high point in the nineteenth chapter where he describes the lifting up of Jesus Christ upon His Cross.

In John 19:28–37, we find the source and the text that reveals to us the heart of the Incarnate God!

> Jesus said: "It is finished!" He bowed his head and gave up his spirit. Since it was the day of preparation, in order to prevent the bodies from remaining on the cross on the Sabbath, for the Sabbath was a high day, the Jews asked Pilate that their limbs might be broken and they may be taken away. So the soldiers came and broke the legs of the first and of the other who had been crucified with Him. But when they came to Jesus and saw that He was already dead, they did not break his legs.
>
> But one of the soldiers pierced His side with a spear and at once there flowed out blood and water. He who saw it has borne witness. His testimony is true and he knows that he tells the truth that you also may believe.
>
> This was done to make the Scripture come true: "Not one of His bones shall be broken" (Exod 12:43, 46). And yet another Scripture says, "They shall look upon Him whom they have pierced" (Zech 12:10).

In this most important passage of his Gospel, St. John solemnly emphasizes three things. First, the fact that Our Lord is already dead when His side is pierced. This fifth wound, therefore, is not properly part of His Passion. It lies beyond. It is pure symbol.

Secondly, His side is pierced, or it is opened and indeed the opening is wide—wide enough to have a hand put within it, wide enough for blood and water to flow freely from it.

Lastly, the prophecy is fulfilled: They shall look on Him whom they have pierced.

With these three points in mind, may we see His Heart just as He sees ours? He awaits us here. May we by His grace get to the depths of the very Truth of the matter.

THE ONLY TRUE LIFE WE HAVE

I remind you of the solemn injunction of the Scriptures: We must look on Him Whom we have pierced. Now, as we look, what do we see? We see, first of all, that moment in time, that historical fact, what became forever the one most important moment in all time—the moment when Jesus Christ, Incarnate Son of God, in His mortal body breathed His last.

This fact of His death is the first thing we affirm by our faith—Christ has died. Without this fact, there is no other. But with it we enter into that Mystery of Faith that ultimately is, in this crisis we are living in, the only hope that our hearts can find.

If it is supremely important that we know that He died, it is equally important that we know *how* He died. At first the cause of His death seems evident, the terrible tortures of His Passion and the agony of the Cross, which is a painful combination. That is how He died, but is it really that evident? St. Mark tells us that Pontius Pilate was surprised that He had died so quickly. Then we remember that He Himself had said: "No one takes my life from me, but I lay it down of my own accord" (Jn 10:18).

If He was stricken in His heart only after He died, it was but a sign of the death that must have come mysteriously from within. He died not so much from His Passion as from His *action*—the action of His heart, that burst from within, which could contain no more that He could give to the world.

This gift of Christ is so supremely important that its revelation cannot be left to private piety. St. John, both here in the Gospel and in his first epistle, made an explicit inventory of what he saw. He tells us that there were three things that issued from His body on the Cross—the spirit that He breathed at the last, and the water and the blood that flowed a little later from His opened side.

It is significant that all four Evangelists describe Christ's death with the same phrase: He gave up His spirit. *Spirit!* What a wondrous mystery in that one word! Human breath is a symbol of that invisible reality we have come to call the human soul. The created spirit of the man Jesus leaves His body as a result of taking His last breath—as it has been for Him and will be for all of us: *death!*

But the man Jesus is a person Who is God, and so the spirit here is another reality as well—the Divine Spirit, the mutual Spirit of the Father and the Son. Into His Father's hands, then, He commends His Spirit.

These, you will remember, were His last spoken words. His human soul, created in Nazareth 33 years before, and His Holy Spirit from eternity. Only by His death could He release His Spirit as He told His Apostles the night before He died: "If I do not go away, the Paraclete will not come to you. If I go, I will send Him to you" (Jn 16:7).

The Holy Spirit of Pentecost is no other than the Holy Spirit of Good Friday—the same Holy Spirit that fashioned Christ's Heart in His mother's womb and that came forth from that Heart upon the Cross. This union of Spirit and Body that is Christ is also the same union that is the Church. Hence, all this recent talk among the fashionable theologians about the disjunction between spirit and body, about the incompatibility between the charismatic and the institutional, it's just so much human invention and vanity.

No, Spirit is not alone in this Paschal Mystery. As St. John insists, there is a three-fold witness: the Spirit, the water, and the blood, and those three are one. That natural fluid in the heart—to use the medical term hydropericardium—is like water, the water St. John saw coming from Christ's open side.

And it is a clear and natural sign. Water is the elemental source of all terrestrial life. In it, all organisms, if we are to live, must in one way or another, swim. It was the same universal symbolism that underlaid the gesture whereby Our Lord began His public ministry as the Spirit's anointed One, when He descended into the Jordan River at the feet of His cousin John the Baptist.

But there was another baptism by which He was to be baptized. From His baptism of water at the beginning, He moved straight to His baptism of blood at the end. And now, at the end, *both* came forth as clear signs from His Heart.

Here is the life and the more abundant life that He had come into the world to give.

I bid you please fulfill once more the prophecy and look upon Him Whom we have pierced. His side is opened and we can see His Heart, broken by the action of His Spirit and pouring out upon us the water and blood of His life.

These are the signs, the sacraments, that He has left to His Church, His Bride. Throughout these grim days in which we now live, let us contemplate the mystery of the sacramental life, for it is the only true life we have—His life and ours.

THE TOTAL OBJECT OF OUR FAITH

The Christ we are contemplating here, and indeed, all our life long, must be the one and only Christ—Jesus Christ yesterday, today, and the same forever.

He is the one Whom we have pierced, but His Heart is as pierced on Easter Sunday as it was on Good Friday. And it will be still just as pierced on the last day when He comes in judgment, as on that evening when St. Thomas put his hand in Jesus' side and said, "My Lord and my God" (Jn 20:27–29). For in the Apocalypse we read, "Behold He is coming with the clouds and every eye will see Him, everyone who pierced Him" (Apoc 1:7).

It is the total Mystery of Faith then that we must contemplate, just as we acclaim that total mystery in the Mass: Christ has died, Christ is risen, Christ will come again. If this brief formula indeed contains the total Mystery of Faith, it is in turn contained in that one action that immediately follows in the Mass—the consecration of the Most Holy Eucharist.

For the Holy Eucharist is, properly speaking, *the* Mystery of Faith. Such are the words of Pope Paul VI in his great encyclical *Mysterium Fidei* that he issued in the course of the Vatican Council. He recalled the importance of certain aspects of Eucharistic doctrine, focusing on the Real Presence of Christ, and the worship due to the Holy Eucharist even outside of Mass.

The Holy Eucharist is not mentioned in the Creed because it is not just a part of the Creed—it is the *whole* Creed. For in it alone, we remember Christ as He wills to be remembered, as He wills to be awaited, and we possess Him as He wills to be possessed.

Here and now in the Holy Eucharist is the *total* Christ. We recall Him from the past here and now as He dies upon His Cross. We bring Him down from Heaven here and now. Risen from the dead, He sits at the right hand of His Father. We anticipate our own death and resurrection as here and now He judges the living and the dead.

This total action of Christ, which is at once the source and content of our faith, is what we call the Paschal Mystery, and it is totally renewed and resumed in the action of each Mass.

We can and do distinguish the two parts of this action. First is that part where Christ goes to His Father, passing out of this world in His death and resurrection and ascension that we call His sacrifice as part of the Mass. Then comes the part where He remains with us, giving us His life as our very food in a sacrament we call the Holy Eucharist.

But the two are integrally one. His movement to His Father and His movement to us are but *the one movement* of His Heart. He cannot go to the Father without us, for we are the completion of His body, and He cannot remain with us without His Father, for in their mutual Holy Spirit, Son and Father are one.

The two actions are thus distinct, but they are inseparable, just as the two commandments of charity are distinct but inseparable in the one Heart of Christ.

Now the Holy Eucharist is indeed the sign of this action of Christ, but in the Mystery of Faith, this sign is perfectly proportioned to the reality that it symbolizes, just as the sacred humanity of self is at once the sign and reality of Christ's being. It is His Real Presence, His very self under the appearances of bread and wine.

The holy Church insists that the surest safeguard of this Mystery of Faith is that the Church celebrate the Feast of Corpus Christi, the liturgical celebration of the Body of Christ.

The presence of Our Lord at the altar is the utmost guarantee of the reality of our entire situation.

He would have us celebrate the solemnity of His Sacred Heart in the week following the solemnity of His Body. The Heart of Jesus now is His Eucharistic Heart—this source and content of His Paschal Mystery—the total object of our faith.

CONTEMPLATING THE MYSTERY OF INIQUITY

It is all very true that the Holy Eucharist is indeed the sign of the action of Christ, but there is something else about the Mystery of Faith that is equally true and we must now ponder it as well. This other truth is that for all the spontaneity of Christ's action, we must see what was done to Him. If His Heart was opened by the force of a lance being thrust into Him, it is equally true that it was opened by the force of hatred toward Him.

We must never forget that the wound in His Heart was opened by the thrust of a spear. Here is His Passion, which is our action—we must indeed look on Him Whom we have pierced.

This is no mere metaphor. The centurion acted, if unwittingly, but yet really, in our name that day, no less than St. John was acting in our name when he was given the bequest of Christ's mother (cf. Jn 19:27).

The fact that Our Lord cannot die again is because of Himself, not because of us. If it were up to us, He would die again. As the epistle to the Hebrews puts it: "They crucify again the Son of God and hold Him up to contempt" (Heb 6:6).

All of this is to say that the Paschal Mystery—the death, resurrection, and ascension of Jesus Christ—is essentially *redemptive*, like the incarnation of Christ, as it has been revealed to us, is essentially redemptive.

The Paschal Mystery presupposed another mystery, what St. Paul has called the Mystery of Iniquity (cf. 2 Thess 2:7). This is the reality of *man's action*—what he has wanted. Here creation has overstepped its boundaries and is challenging God's creation in calling for God's *re-creation* or redemption.

I really believe we should contemplate this mystery if we are to truly see the signs of the times, and contemplate it deep within our hearts.

It's mysterious of course, but no less serious. It is precisely the filth of moral evil that we see being offered to us. This inclination to evil, this concupiscence which St. John described as the concupiscence of the flesh, the concupiscence of the eyes, and the pride of life, is not just a thing. An actual thing can only be something that we will. Yes, the concupiscence leads to actual things that we know so well, and as Our Lord described so vividly: lust, theft, murder, greed, fornication, malice, adultery, envy, slander, indecency, pride, folly—all these things that came from original sin, that original sin actually committed by Adam and naturally inherited by all his descendants (cf. *Catechism of the Catholic Church*, pt. 3, no. 2514).

Perhaps it is a more significant sign of our times that the fundamental doctrine of original sin has been equivocated, minimized, and not to say, even denied, by those who still call themselves Christians.

What greater peril is there than to deny the peril?

What greater sin is there than to say there is no sin?

What greater wound is there than to feel the wounds from sin in our hearts and yet see no wounds in Christ for the sins we have committed?

In our contemplation of the Mystery of Iniquity, we must take care not to enter into our own hearts and simply stay there. There are features of this mystery that Our Lord has revealed to us that are more mysterious still, that are touching us in our hearts here and now and touching the very edges of eternity.

Behind the original sin on earth looms a primordial sin in the cosmos. Behind the individual will of the creature called man lurks the unbounding will of the greatest creature of all—a pure spirit, so imaging God that it claimed to be God.

And so we have the creator of evil, the father of lies. This Satanic presence is utterly and grimly real. Without it, the entire revelation of the New Testament is completely unintelligible. Indeed, the sure sign of counterfeit Christianity is to deny that Christianity can have a counterfeit—that Christ can have an enemy so personal going after His Heart, seeking the corruption of man, and seeking the naming of himself as god.

We can feel him, yes, for on our road to Christ Himself, this fearsome spirit has power to destroy us and take our soul and body to Hell—*if we but let him.*

The notion of Hell—that mysterious reality prepared for the devil and his angels—reminds us in this moment of crisis how well we need this reminder, of the true dimensions of our destiny. For better or for worse, we are caught up with the angels of God.

Here is the Mystery of Iniquity in its true dimension and correlative with redemption. Thus, God's purposes are served even by him who refused to serve.

If in no other way we can see Christ for what He is, look at him whom Christ Himself described as the "strong man." There you will see better the Strong Man that is Christ Himself.

Look first into your heart, and then look at the enemy who has entry there. Your contemplation must not end here, however. If you really contemplate, you will see in your misery, and in his malice, *the mystery of the mercy of God.*

This merciful God, Who is Himself wounded, this merciful God—Who has been through His Passion bound by our sins before He could manifest His action of the superabounding grace of his love.

WOUNDING HIS SACRED HEART WITH OUR SINS

As we face the two mysteries of our existence, the Mystery of Iniquity and the Mystery of Faith, we should see more clearly than ever before that reality that is the Gospel. I refer to the first spoken words of Our Lord in his public ministry as quoted by St. Mark: "The time is fulfilled, and the Kingdom of God is at hand. Repent!" (4:17).

Repentance, *confessio*, *metanoia*—all of these are the same reality—the reality of a changed heart, a heart that turns from itself to that which is at once wholly *beyond* itself, wholly within the Heart of God and Him Incarnate.

This repentance is for all, for all have sinned. And in the Heart of the Creator and Redeemer, there is room for all. The entrance into that Heart, as we should now indeed know, is opened wide. When we speak in this fashion, we are again speaking the literal truth. There is no indulgence of metaphor when we speak of His Heart, just as His action from within and His Passion from without are real, so too must be *our* action and *our* passion now.

What we do and what is done to us, what we give and what we receive, can be so because He has once more anticipated us in His mercy. He has provided that certain of these actions and sufferings on our part can be the real and efficacious sign of our repentance and our gift from Him of pardon. I am referring of course to the great sign of His mercy, whereby He has sacramentalized penance and made it His own action shared with ours.

That three-fold action of ours, called contrition, confession, and satisfaction, is joined to that action of His of absolution — and we have the Sacrament of Penance and reconciliation and peace. What a gift we have here in this sacrament! It is the perfect renewal of our baptism and the perfect preparation for the Holy Eucharist.

And just as much as this is a certainty of God's pardon, it is, if we think upon it, the necessity of our confession. Yes, the confession of all mortal sins is necessary for the remission of any of them. This confession, preceded of course by contrition and followed by satisfaction, is after all the least we can do on our part in this mysterious sharing that is the sign of our repentance and His pardon.

How strangely fitting it is then that the Holy Church has been so paradoxically criticized for this sacrament. On the one hand, she is said to be too lenient as she guarantees forgiveness. On the other hand, she is said to be too strict as she demands confession.

Such criticism betrays an ignorance not only of the ways of God, but also of the ways of man. Now it can only be this ignorance surely which explains the very noticeable decline in the use of this sacrament in recent years.

Too many Catholics have been with the world too much, for evidently, they share the world's view regarding the mysteries we speak of. As for the Mystery of Iniquity, there is no such thing they say. Then there's the guilt complex, too gruesome to be true. Let's not impede our evolutionary progress to perfection by feeling guilty about our sins!

And as for the Mystery of Faith, that too is an idle dream. It really is too good to be true. For why would God care to bother with the likes of us?

Seemingly contradictory in their starting point of optimism and pessimism, they really come to the same conclusion: the self-subsistence of man is alienation from God and thus becomes the ultimate despair of man.

Is it not just possible that this attitude among Catholics toward confession, at least implicitly, is the very surest sign of our times—the sign of our desperate need to see things as they are? And things as they are can be summarized as two facts: the sinfulness of man and the mercy of God. Or they can be summarized as two mysteries: the Mystery of Iniquity and the Mystery of Faith.

What I have noted here is applicable to us all. Indeed, it is more applicable to those of us who regard ourselves, or are regarded by others, as "good people."

The confession of mortal sins is not really so much in question here, as is the confession of *venial sins*—you know, the sins of the "good people," those sins that admittedly do not have to be confessed to be forgiven.

What about such sins, and what about such people who commit them? Well, the Sacrament of Penance is there awaiting them. By the firm and constant teaching of the Church, the sacramental confession and absolution of venial sins is especially pleasing to Our Lord—fulfilling His desire in instituting this sacrament as the privileged sign of *our misery* and *His mercy* meeting in peace.

You will remember that in His words of institution, *He speaks of sin as sin, with no distinction.* Is this not really the sense of His complaint revealed to His saints that He feels more clearly than all others the *sins of His friends*? Hatred and contempt are more bearable than ingratitude and neglect. He wants that we are either cold or hot. Because we are neither, He will vomit us from His mouth (cf. Apoc 3:15–16).

Or as His prophet Zechariah saw, "What are these wounds in the midst of thy hands?" And He will answer: "With these I was wounded in the house of those who loved Me" (Zech 13:6).

The continuing of venial sin and the neglect of his Sacrament of Penance are what hurt Him most in His Sacred Heart.

For we must remember that the wound in His Heart was not caused by the lance thrust into Him, but by one of the curious onlookers who was simply there at Calvary checking on Him, *one of us*—the scourge marks and the spittle of hatred are gone and forgotten but the spear mark of indifference remains.

THE LIVING, PULSING HEART OF JESUS CHRIST

We see our own need for penance in response to our own actions of sin and to His actions of grace. This turning from our heart to His Heart is at once the least and the most we can do.

But we must see more clearly what this turning to Him really means. After contrition and confession comes satisfaction, that third integral part of the Sacrament of Penance. Symbolically, it means an act of charity or tiny prayers imposed by the priest. But really, it *should mean* our entire life thereafter.

By this addition of comity, profoundly proportioned to our nature, the remission of guilt does not necessarily mean the remission of pain. The forgiven sinner is not the same as one who never sinned. This is but a synchroneity to that Mystery of Faith wherein we see the Risen Christ still bearing His wounds. *We must repair those wounds.* We must make up what is lacking in His suffering for the completion of His Body. This making-up, this reparation, we must do all our life long until that hour comes when we shall share His death—the final mortification for here completed that prepares us for paradise and our own resurrection at last.

This program of life in death, of love in suffering, of ecstasy in endurance, of joy in pain, is completely and totally the program of the Gospel. It is good news indeed. Here is our rule of life in a world in crisis, and its sign, once more, is the sign of His Heart.

Can we make this rule more specific now, more applicable to our everyday lives? What specifically must we do now that our baptism is renewed by penance and our future progressively unfolds before us as our present? It would be unwise to attempt anything really specific here, as each of our lives has its own incommunicable character, its opportunities and perils for oneself alone.

However, there is one item in this rule that can be—must be—common to us all, shared by all the members of the Body of Christ but remaining at the same time the most personal and intimate communion with Christ alone.

This one item, as you might have already surmised, is the Holy Eucharist—that one reality that we must come back to, and come back to, throughout all our lives.

The Blessed Sacrament of the Body of Christ—it is for all of us together, for it makes us to *be* His Body, members with members until we all obtain the unity of grace, and the knowledge of the Son of God, to mature manhood, to the measure of the stature of the fullness of Christ.

But for each of us individually, it is likewise true. Here is our life—the program of our reparation and our preparation, from day to day until for us time is no more.

There is a very apt simile in this instance, taken from the biology of our own bodies, that illustrates to near perfection the meaning of the Holy Eucharist in ordinary life.

In the human body there is only one kind of blood, but there are two very different aspects or phases of that blood in two corresponding kinds of blood vessels. There is the blood as it flows *from* the heart through the vessels called arteries, to all the members of the body. And then there is the blood that flows from the members through the vessels called the veins back *to* the heart.

The blood in the veins is dark red, laden with impurities, to be purified by the heart and exhaled by the lungs. Thus renewed, this same blood is now in the arteries, bright red, with oxygen to give life to the body. And so the blood circulates through the heart in a ceaseless rhythm of reparation and renewal.

Thus it is, with the Holy Eucharist and us. We come to the altar to give ourselves to God in the Holy Eucharist that is the sacrifice of Christ's Body. We come to the altar as living members—but as barely living—*not* with the guilt of sin upon us, but with its *pain*.

Our poor cells are dark red, but the Heart of Jesus needs these poor cells to be given to Him if He is to renew His Body. And renew it He does, for from the altar, we receive Christ into us in the Holy Eucharist that is the communion of His Body. We ourselves are now in the presence of Christ; bright red, His Heart beats within us, giving us His life, and so in the daily cycle of reparation and preparation, from sacrifice to communion, and from communion to sacrifice, our lives are lived.

Do you not see now more clearly the absolute centrality of the Holy Eucharist in the whole program of our life as willed by God and as He created in His Gospel?

In such a program, the details are unimportant and everything is but a detail compared with this: *absolutely central* to the Holy Eucharist—without which it is but an empty sign—is the *reality* of the living pulsing Heart of Jesus Christ.

AN AWESOME RESPONSIBILITY AND A WONDROUS CLAIM

The Eucharistic journey in the cadence of our lives will, of course, someday have an end. This is only for this earth, and someday the veil of the Eucharistic appearances to us will be drawn away and we shall see the Lord as He is.

It is this end that orders all that precedes it and gives our earthly lives the sense we are to have if we are to have any sense at all. That sense is simply *holiness* which means to be with God, to be what He created us to be, set apart from nothingness and totally here with Him.

This radical sense of the holy is perhaps best imaged in the recurring scriptural figure of the Temple—the Temple in

Jerusalem, the place toward which all Israel journeyed—the place where God's people met their God.

But that Temple was only the figure of Christ's Body. The sanctuary veil was rent at the moment when the real sanctuary was revealed to us—the Sacred Heart of Jesus opened on the Cross. From that open Heart, we have seen flow the sacraments of the Church. We must now see more closely those sacraments which sanctify us, to make us truly sacred, to make us be with God amidst His people.

The first and most fundamental sacrament, without which no other can be received and the Temple remains closed, is baptism. This is the water from the well of his Heart that He had promised—the water springing up into life everlasting.

Now the sacrament whereby this happens is also everlasting. Even if this life should be lost to mortal sin, the baptized person remains baptized, a Christian, a member of Christ's Body, a child of God. That is why this sacrament can never be repeated. It is indelible.

Sanctifying grace is only the second effect of baptism and, of course, it can be lost. But the first effect cannot be lost, and that is the mysterious mark or seal of the sacrament whereby one is forever a member of the people of God—the Holy Church, and has, therefore, some mysterious claim on sanctifying grace by right.

Thus, even as a sinner, the baptized Christian is holy. And for better or worse, remains thus sealed for eternity.

From the earliest age of the Church, baptism has been conferred on infants, and this custom of the Church is profoundly correct. Baptism is essentially the sacrament of infancy. Although its potentiality is the active Christian life of faith, hope, and charity, it is for the child simply to receive, then to receive the other sacraments and to grow as a child in the life of God.

If baptism is for infants, and we can only receive it once, it must be somehow confirmed—ratified—enabling the Christian to *give as well as to receive* once he has reached spiritual adulthood.

This first and necessary sacrament has been reaffirmed by Christ, for there is in the Church a second sacrament, called, appropriately, confirmation—a second seal upon us, the indelible seal of adulthood in the Body of Christ.

The confirmed Christian is one who gives as well as receives, showing maturely his faith, hope, and charity with the members of his family, the people of God. Both his responsibilities and his claims are thus compounded because when much has been put into him by God, much will be expected of him to give to others. And what is expected is giving witness to the world of the holiness of God.

The confirmed Christian gives his witness by the holiness of the temple that is himself, reflecting all that he believes by the light and warmth of the Sacred Heart of Jesus that he bears.

Thirdly, there is a sacrament of sanctification that is a total organism of the Body of Christ. I'm speaking of ultimate giving from which all others receive. This sacrament is called holy orders by which bishops, priests, and deacons, all in their proper order, administer to the people of God the one eternal priesthood of Jesus Christ.

The priest is the minister of that Word and that Sacrament that is Christ. He serves as Christ's other self in the sanctuary of the Temple. He brings God to His people and the people to their God. He is himself, of course, a member of the people and as such he must receive as they do the same one priesthood of Christ. His own priesthood therefore is not for himself but for others. It is an indelible seal for exclusively giving—the giving to others of the life of God.

In this deepest sense then, every priest is equally holy. His one claim on Christ's Heart as a priest is the claim of his office—not to receive, but to give.

If the sense of our earthly life is essentially our holiness with God, our eternal destiny into Heaven must be honored. We must remember that our journey to holiness here is indeed but a beginning. We are not there yet.

By virtue of the three sacraments—baptism, confirmation, and holy orders—the sacred is staked out in this world, but only as a kind of beachhead, and out from that beachhead, we must deal with some skirmishes. And so to help us, we have the sacramentals—places and things that by the authority of Christ, the Church has made holy.

But in the world as it is, the world in the secular sense as touched by grace and corrupted by the enemy, there is surely a need of a further sign—a sign from God that He has indeed committed Himself regarding this creation, something called *Good*. By His love, which is His grace, He made created love to be an efficacious sign of that grace.

Sure enough, as we have seen, that need has already been fulfilled by Christ's institution. There is a sacrament of this world issuing from the Heart of Jesus and endowed with His own grace and charity, the most intimate and basic relationship in natural human life, namely, the bond of marriage.

The union of man and woman as being a mutual completion of body and personality is almost an obvious reality as it is by being the means of perpetuating the species itself. Those two realities of marriage—the realities of complementarity and procreation—are absolutely primordial to our nature.

The fact that they are not some mere accidental arrangement but rather the deliberate design of the Creator, something we did not have to learn from the revelation of the Scriptures. But the fact that they *are* revealed adds immeasurably to the significance of their truth.

Think of it. From the very beginning, God had in mind the significance of two in one flesh. It was to be the sign of human love at its very best—at once instinctively simple and the most aspiring ideal. Here is the perfect giving and receiving, and because it is perfect, it is creative.

Because Our Lord gave us these sacraments, we must reflect on our corresponding responsibilities. We must pray therefore that we may be worthy—not just of Christ's promises of the hereafter but of *His need here and now*. He has put upon us, and forever, the seal of His Heart.

It is an awesome responsibility, but it is also a wondrous claim.

DEVOTION TO THE SACRED HEART OF JESUS

Devotion to the Sacred Heart of Jesus is not just another devotion in the tradition of the Church. Mother Church has an ample cupboard and all sorts of treasures are in there. But among all the devotions, the one to Our Lord's Sacred Heart is the most unique one.

The clearest sign of Our Lord's Sacred Heart is precisely the Sacred Liturgy, the Holy Sacrifice of the Mass. In the judgement of the Magisterium of the Church, the feast day celebrating the Sacred Heart reminds us that the Sacred Heart is actually coterminous with the history of the Church herself. This devotion to the Sacred Heart is as old as the Church. The best proof of that is the Gospel of St. John.

St. Margaret Mary had something to do with advancing this devotion to the Sacred Heart among the people at large as a specific object of adoration and total prayer. But it goes back to St. John's Gospel (Jn 19:34–37). And he swears that it is true! It's not, therefore, some kind of figment of the mind or a myth. It's a fact! The fact of what? The fact of His death! Our Lord was wounded in His side *after He had died*. He didn't really suffer then, did He? Ah, but He did!

It was said that the water and blood coming out of His side was from His Heart—but it was a rupture of His Heart. You can almost truly say that *He died of a broken heart*. He offered His Heart to us because His Heart was His life! Up until these recent years we have presumed that death meant precisely that—when the heart stops, death occurs. The symbol remains and it remains ineffaceable.

In all cultures the heart is a singular unique organ of the body. It is the core of Our Lord's life, and it was already spilled out, which means that the Sacred Heart of Jesus is pure symbol. It was not efficacious for His Heart to participate in the redemption, as did His other wounds on His hands and His feet and the innumerable slashings on His back and His front by the scourging. You could almost say that He couldn't feel the lance being thrust into His Heart—but He felt it already—He did not need that lance. That only made it manifest to us, to the historian John, that indeed He died, assuring from the Scriptures that they would not break His bones but would pierce His Heart.

And so we have this remarkable fact of God's own invention — the power of the Holy Spirit to say: "What can I leave to the world to show how much I loved the world? How much I loved My people? Not only Israel but *all* the people all over the world, the gentiles and the dimensions of this number that cannot be measured?" It's infinite — because it's God Who died. You know there is one divine person, and the Sacred Heart of Jesus is perhaps the best authentication of that reality.

When we focus on believing what the Holy Spirit showed to us in the Sacred Heart, we're not looking at some abstract statement by an ecumenical council using Greek metaphysical terms of person and nature and all that sort of thing. Important and as fundamental as that all is, it had to be enunciated to show us that really, the Heart, the Heart of Christ, surpasses words. Our Lord did not just speak to us from His mouth with all the words in the four Gospels. *He now speaks to us from His Heart.*

And what came out of His Heart? Blood and water from that little chalice of His Heart, giving His last drop of blood for us.

This is what this means for us — by the sheer *action* of the Holy Spirit, this devotion just grew for us through the centuries in the Church. St. Margaret Mary does deserve some kind of special recognition to be sure. She's a canonized saint, which means that whatever she did in her work for the Church is authenticated. It's really backed up and guaranteed by an infallible Church.

There's no need for a definition of faith in the matter. It's already been defined by the Ecumenical Council of Chalcedon in 451, which was pivotal in defining the dual nature of Christ as *both human and divine*, and addressed several disputes about His nature. From this Council, we have the symbol of His Heart that transcends the words of the Canon of the Mass — the symbol which we see and the symbol we should feel.

Heart to heart, which happens to be the motto that the great Cardinal Newman adopted for himself. *Cor ad cor loquitur*: "Heart speaks to heart."

This is what we need to celebrate, this living Sacred Heart of Jesus, ever since that first Easter Sunday. This Heart is still beating, but it's still wounded too. Our Lord saw to that on Easter and a few days later He said to St. Thomas: "Thomas, put your hand into my Heart" (Jn 20:26–27). Put your finger in my hand and put your hand in my Heart—not just your finger, Thomas, but your hand in my Heart. It's that big a gap—a wound that you can touch!

And so, into eternity, Jesus has this open Heart—*a Sacred Heart which is now alive.* It better be alive because it is *our life*—it's the only life we have, because Jesus in His human nature is sanctifying grace personified—the grace of the Holy Spirit, this is Jesus.

To put our life all together so that we can grasp it well, is His Heart. Down through the years, from Pius X to Benedict XVI, all the popes have been speaking to us about the Sacred Heart—always making the need for our devotion to it more intense, so to speak.

There were two great encyclicals the popes wrote to help us understand the importance and need for true devotion to the Sacred Heart. First there was *Miserentissimus Redemptor* (On the Sacred Heart of Jesus) of Pius XI in 1928. Then Pope Pius XII wrote *Haurietis aquas* in 1956, beginning with the line from the prophet Isaiah (12:3): "You shall draw waters with joy out of the Savior's fountain."

Pope John Paul II, in his first encyclical, *Redemptor Hominis* (The Redeemer of Man) in 1979, wrote almost exclusively and totally a meditation on the heart. He brings a fuller understanding of the human person and of Christ, focusing on the humanity of the Mystery of Redemption and how Christ truly reveals Himself to man in a union of love with each and every person.

So we have no more excuses not to be aware of this truth. We should make the most of it as Our Lord expects us to—He's done His part and His Mother Mary, you may be sure, has done her part too. The Sacred Heart of the Son and the Immaculate Heart of His Mother are placed back to back on the Church's calendar of feast days. And that is the way it is now by the judgment of the Church and the way it should be.

Let us ask Our Lord for this great grace, this great grace of a tremendous reality of His Sacred Heart, as our prayer always. Our first prayer of the day with our morning offering should be to ask Jesus to take us to live within His Sacred Heart. That is *where we must live* on our journey to Heaven.

WHAT JESUS PROMISED US

Jesus Himself promised us that we can live within His Sacred Heart and He welcomes us to come dwell there. He told this to St. Margaret Mary Alacoque in the seventeenth century, beginning with His first appearance to her on December 27, 1673, and continuing through June 1675. Her death came on October 17, 1690, at the age of 43. She wrote a short devotional work, *La Devotion au Sacre-Coeur de Jesus* (Devotion to the Sacred Heart of Jesus) which was published posthumously by J. Croiset in 1698.

St. Margaret Mary, canonized on May 13, 1920, by Pope Benedict XV, was a Visitation nun and mystic living in a monastery in Paray-le-Monial, Burgundy, in the Kingdom of France. A humble, kind, and patient woman, she suffered many trials to test whether her vocation was genuine, but she had made a childhood promise to the Blessed Mother to devote her life to Jesus, who she first encountered scourged and bloody when she was a young woman. He appeared to her to admonish her after a night of carnival partying and dancing. She then remembered her promise to the Blessed Mother to consecrate herself to religious life.

When Jesus first appeared to her in the monastery two days after Christmas in 1673, He allowed her to rest her head upon His Heart. Then He explained to her the wonders of His love and told her He wanted her to make this known to all mankind so that all could share in the treasures of His goodness.

He said He chose her for His work to make His Sacred Heart known to everyone.

Throughout 1674 and into the spring of 1675, Jesus continued to visit St. Margaret Mary and in those visits spoke to her about how sad He was. As she explained:

> Jesus spoke of the sadness He feels because *His great love for humanity* receives in exchange "nothing but ingratitude and indifference, coldness and contempt." And this "is more grievous to Me than all that I endured in My Passion."

He gave to her over the course of several apparitions the devotion to His Sacred Heart, the Devotion of receiving Holy Communion on the first Fridays of each month for nine months as an act of reparation, and the Great Promises for those who are devoted to His Sacred Heart. He also explained to her the need for Eucharistic Adoration and Holy Hours and that He wished everyone to participate in these activities frequently.

To St. Margaret Mary, Jesus made Twelve Promises to show us in no uncertain terms how much He wants us to devote ourselves to His Most Sacred Heart. For those who do, He promised:

1. I will give them all the graces necessary in their state of life.
2. I will establish peace in their homes.
3. I will comfort them in all their afflictions.
4. I will be their secure refuge during life, and above all, in death.
5. I will bestow abundant blessings upon all their undertakings.
6. Sinners will find in My Heart the source and infinite ocean of mercy.
7. Lukewarm souls shall become fervent.
8. Fervent souls shall quickly mount to high perfection.
9. I will bless every place in which an image of My Heart is exposed and honored.
10. I will give to priests the gift of touching the most hardened hearts.

11. Those who shall promote this devotion shall have their names written in My Heart.
12. I promise you in the excessive mercy of My Heart that My all-powerful love will grant to all those who receive Holy Communion on the First Fridays in nine consecutive months the grace of final perseverance; they shall not die in My disgrace, nor without receiving their sacraments. My divine Heart shall be their safe refuge in this last moment.

We can live within His Sacred Heart. He welcomes us there. Throughout our days let us pray to Him Who loves us with our own little prayers from *our* hearts. "Most Sacred Heart of Jesus, have mercy on me, a sinner." "Jesus, I trust in you!" We must begin each day by telling Him how much we love Him, simply because He loves us so much!

REFLECTIONS FROM THE SAINTS

"If only I could put into everybody's heart the fire I have in my breast, which makes me burn with such love for the Heart of Jesus and the Heart of Mary." —ST. JACINTA MARTO

"And He [Christ] showed me that it was His great desire of being loved by men and of withdrawing them from the path of ruin that made Him want to manifest His Heart to men, with all the treasures of love, of mercy, of grace, of sanctification and salvation which it contains, in order that those who desire to render Him and procure Him all the honor and love possible might themselves be abundantly enriched with those divine treasures of which His Heart is the source." —ST. MARGARET MARY ALACOQUE

"The Divine Heart is an ocean full of all good things, wherein poor souls can cast all their needs; it is an ocean full of joy to drown all our sadness, an ocean of humility to drown our folly, an ocean of mercy to those in distress, an ocean of love in which to submerge our poverty." —ST. MARGARET MARY ALACOQUE

"O Sacred Heart of Jesus, fountain of eternal life, Your Heart is a glowing furnace of Love. You are my refuge and my sanctuary… [W]e are weak, but by the Heart of Jesus we shall become strong; by the charity of the Heart of Jesus, we shall triumph over death and Hell, and in the Heart of Jesus we shall find all the treasures of wisdom and knowledge." —ST. GERTRUDE THE GREAT

"Surely it is a source of profound consolation to know that we are loved so deeply by Our Lord, who constantly carries us in His Heart." —ST. FRANCIS DE SALES

"What joy one experiences when one abandons oneself into the arms of Jesus! The faithful soul becomes His dearest child. He opens His arms to receive it and presses it to His Most Sacred Heart." —ST. GEMMA GALGANI

CHAPTER TEN

WHY WE NEED A RULE OF LIFE

"So I say to you: Ask, and it will be given to you; search, and you will find; knock, and the door will be opened to you. For the one who asks always receives; the one who searches always finds; the one who knocks will always have the door opened to him" (*Lk 11:9–10*).

WHY DO WE NEED A PERSONAL RULE OF Life? On our journey to live within the Sacred Heart of Jesus, a Rule of Life that leads us to practice daily devotions, read and meditate on Scripture, receive the Holy Eucharist and the Sacrament of Penance, and orient our entire lives to focus on Our Lord, is the surest way to keep walking on the rocky, narrow path that leads to Heaven.

This Rule is addressed to all laymen and women who are aware that, simply as human beings, they have received from God a *call to holiness*, and who, as Catholics, recognize their mission to defend and spread the Faith that comes to us from the Apostles, presented and explained by Holy Mother Church in her Teaching Office. It is therefore addressed to all who have received the gift of the Faith and who acknowledge that the gift imposes three duties on all who receive it: to let it entirely form their lives and govern their actions, to make it understood and loved by others, and to hand it down intact to the next generation.

There are always two "poles" in the following of Christ: faith and works, the contemplative and the active life, the spiritual and the practical, love of God and love of neighbor, separating from the world and leavening it, going out, ascending and descending the ladder seen by Jacob "standing upon the earth and the top thereof touching Heaven" (Gen 28:12).

It is enough to recall two teachings of Our Lord: His word to Martha, busy with preparations for feeding the hungry, that Mary had chosen the better part (cf. Lk 10:42); and His description of the Last Judgment which seems to say that the sole criterion will be the actual doing of works of mercy, even perhaps exclusively the corporal works of mercy (cf. Mt 25:32–46). Evidently the Son of God does not contradict Himself—and in these two teachings He wants us to know for sure that love of God, whenever it is genuine, necessarily fills the heart with a love for all His children and with a longing to be of service to them and thus to Him.

The mode of service depends on the individual "word" spoken by God to each individual soul. St. Thérèse of Lisieux, burning with love of God in her cloister, wished for martyrdom, and longed to be a missionary to the whole world and to bring to it the tender ministrations of her Lord. Some are especially called to the contemplative life, others to the so-called active life. The vocation of the laity is pre-eminently a mixed vocation—a vocation to both poles in the following of Christ.

Our Savior said, "I am the door. If anyone enters by me he shall be safe and shall go in and out, and shall find pasture.... I am come that they may have life" (Jn 10:7, 9–10). And He has said, "He that abides in me, and I in him, the same bears much fruit: for without me you can do nothing.... In this is my Father glorified—that you bring forth very much fruit and become my disciples" (Jn 15:4, 8).

Every day (how many times?) we pray, "Hallowed be Thy name." By what means is our Father's name to be glorified? By our doing His will and bringing forth very much fruit as disciples of Jesus Christ whom He has sent. And how are we to bring forth very much fruit? By abiding in Him, and He in us. And how is this to be? By eating His Flesh and drinking His Blood.

We are to go in and out—going into prayer always to the inner chamber in secret, to the Holy Sacrifice and the Holy Eucharist as often as may be, there to draw living waters from the fountains of the Savior (cf. Isa 12:3); and going out, to be channels of that living water to the parched and gasping world. By the command of Christ, that is the vocation of each member of the laity.

To refuse a recognized call from Him is to refuse Him. "If any man abides not in me, he shall be cast forth as a branch, and shall wither, and they shall gather him up, and cast him into the fire; and he burns" (Jn 15:6). We do well to take seriously these fearful words recorded by the great Apostle of Love.

In our present time, as in the past, there has been much fruitless argument as to whether a man is to be saved by faith or by good works—a useless argument, since faith without works is a dead faith, that is, no true faith at all. So today there is much fruitless argument about the personal aspect of religion versus the community aspect, about love of God versus love of neighbor, about the "vertical" aspect versus the "horizontal" aspect.

The argument is vain because it is not possible for a person to have a deep and genuine love of God, making union with Him the goal of life, and yet to be indifferent to His commandment that we are to "love one another as I have loved you" (Jn 15:12). It was the specific prayer of Jesus Christ, our one great High Priest, "that they all may be one: as Thou, Father, in me, and I in Thee... I in them and Thou in me, that they may be made perfect in one" (Jn 17:21, 23).

Members of the laity are called to a total love of God and, in that love, so to love the world and to do all each person can to help bring to it the only begotten Son Whom the Father sent to rescue and redeem everyone. All works of mercy are ultimately this: the giving of Christ to others.

WHAT CAN WE DO TO HELP IN CHRIST'S MISSION?

"To do all we can to help. . . ." What can we do? What are we obliged to do? This small Rule, in a very simple form, tries to indicate the Church's answer to that question.

"Behold I come: in the head of the book it is written of me that I should do Thy will, O God" (Ps 39:8). Through those words of the psalmist, the Messiah, Our Lord Jesus Christ, offers Himself unceasingly to God the Father.

"Lord, what wouldst Thou have me do?" (Acts 9:6). Thus St. Paul makes his immediate loving submission to God the Son.

"Be it done to me according to Thy word" (Lk 1:38) is the utterance by which and through which the Holy Virgin surrenders herself to the overshadowing of the Holy Spirit.

And all are included in the words Our Savior taught us to pray: "Thy will be done" (Mt 6:10).

The Second Vatican Council told us, and the popes have been telling us insistently ever since, that God has an ascertainable will for His laity—that He has called us, has given us a mission, to serve Him in His Church and among His people. In the Decrees of the Apostolate of the Laity (*Apostolicam actuositatem*) and the Dogmatic Constitution on the Church (*Lumen gentium*), the Council said explicitly that the laity "are called by God to exercise their apostolate to the world like leaven" (AA no. 2) to help "spread the kingdom of Christ throughout the world for the glory of God the Father" (AA no. 1); to "go forth as powerful heralds of a faith in things to be hoped for, provided they steadfastly join to their profession of faith a life springing from faith" (LG no. 35; cf. Heb 11:1).

Thus the Council assigned a mission to the laity, and it is inseparable from—and dependent on—a full response to the universal vocation to holiness. "The success of the lay apostolate depends on the laity's living union with Christ, in keeping with the Lord's words, 'He who abides in me and I in him bears much fruit; for without me you can do nothing'" (AA no. 4; cf. Jn 15:5).

The Council documents speak of how this indispensable living union with Christ is to be sought, and the apostolate fulfilled. If we cull some of the key words and phrases and bring them together, they teach us that it is the God-willed vocation of every Catholic man and woman:

> To live the spirit of the Gospel
> With the ardor of the spirit of Christ;
> In a living union with Christ,
> By participation in the liturgy, learning
> To do all things in the name of the Lord Jesus
> In a continual exercise of faith, hope and charity:
> By faith and by
> Meditation on the word of God, learning
> To seek His will in every event, and
> To see Christ in everyone;
> To do good to all men, especially
> To those of the household of the Faith;
> And nourished by the charity of God,
> To express the true spirit of the Beatitudes in their lives.

As the fathers of Vatican Council II stated in *Lumen gentium* (no. 39):

> The Church, whose mystery is set forth by this sacred Council, is held, as a matter of faith, to be unfailingly holy. This is because Christ, the Son of God, Who with the Father and Spirit is hailed as "alone holy," loved the Church as His Bride, giving Himself up for her so as to sanctify her (cf. Eph 5:25–26); He joined her to Himself as His body and endowed her with the gift of the Holy Spirit for the glory of God. Therefore, all in the Church, whether they belong to the hierarchy or are cared for by it, are called to holiness, according to the Apostle's saying: "For this is the will of God, your sanctification" (1 Thess 4:3; cf. Eph 1:4). This holiness of the Church is constantly shown forth in the fruits of grace which the Spirit produces in the faithful, and so it must be....

These words of the Second Vatican Council, introducing its momentous "call to holiness" as the first and most important agendum in its program of renewal for the Church, most fittingly introduces this Rule of Life for Catholics who wish to grow in personal holiness as they strive to live within the Sacred Heart of Jesus. Catholic laity have a duty to support, defend, and advance the efforts of the Teaching Church. Therefore, each one of us must ground our individual apostolates in a serious pursuit of that personal holiness without which all apostolic labor is in vain.

That the vocation to holiness is not reserved to only a few in the Church but is directly willed by Christ for *all* His members, and that therefore the laity as such is integrally involved by obligation and by right in the Church's life and work, is the emphatic teaching of the Council:

> It is therefore quite clear that all Christians in any state or walk of life are called to the fullness of Christian life and to the perfection of love, and by this holiness a more human manner of life is fostered also in earthly society. In order to reach this perfection, the faithful should use the strength dealt out to them by Christ's gift, so that, following in His footsteps and conformed to His image, doing the will of God in everything, they may wholeheartedly devote themselves to the glory of God and to the service of their neighbor. (Ibid., no. 40)

The Council goes on to describe this holiness, which is *necessary and possible* for Christ's faithful. It limits its description to a few broad statements, which it then briefly applies to three kinds of vocation—clerical, religious, and lay—in the Church:

> The forms and tasks of life are many, but holiness is one—that sanctity which is cultivated by all who act under God's Spirit and, obeying the Father's voice and adoring God the Father in spirit and in truth, follow Christ poor, humble, and cross-bearing, that they may deserve to be partakers of His glory. Each one, however, according to his own gifts and duties, must steadfastly advance along the way of living faith, which arouses hope and works through love. (Ibid., no. 41)

The purpose of this Rule of Life is to follow through on this directive of Vatican II by making more specific what it means for a Catholic lay person to live a *holy* life. The Council itself (and especially its Constitution on the Church, *Lumen gentium*) remains the primary source for this Rule. The

Council called the laity to various apostolates (especially in the Decree on the Laity, *Apostolicam actuositatem*). Yet this Rule also recalls the whole two-thousand-year-old tradition of Catholic spirituality antecedent to and flowing into Vatican II.

As *Apostolicam actuositatem* (no. 2) states:

> The Church was founded to spread the kingdom of Christ over all the earth for the glory of God the Father, to make all men partakers in redemption and salvation and through them to establish the right relationship of the entire world to Christ. Every activity of the Mystical Body with this in view goes by the name of "apostolate"; the Church exercises it through all its members, though in various ways. In fact, the Christian vocation is, of its nature, a vocation to the apostolate as well. In the organism of a living body, no member plays a purely passive part, sharing in the life of the body, it shares at the same time in its activity.
>
> The same is true for the Body of Christ, the Church: "The whole Body achieves full growth in dependence on the full functioning of each part" (Eph 4:16). Between the members of this Body there exists, further, such a unity and solidarity (cf. Eph 4:16) that a member who does not work at the growth of the Body to the extent of his possibilities must be considered useless both to the Church and to himself.

Therefore, our mission in life is to wholeheartedly devote oneself to the glory of God and the service of the neighbor, steadily to advance along the way of living faith, which arouses hope and works through love. How can we fulfill this call of Christ and His Church? This little Rule, in simple form, endeavors to answer that question. To all members of the laity, it strives to show how they can at least begin to live the totality of the Gospel in the totality of their lives.

Being a member of the laity is a beautiful vocation! To grow in holiness by embracing what the Church is asking of each of us individually is our goal. Through His Church God has disclosed His general will for us; we beg Him to hasten the day when we lay men and women, in increasing numbers, will rise from our deep sleep and step forward to accept our assigned parts in God's program for mankind.

The infinite God, in presenting Himself to our finite minds and foolish hearts, does so under numerous aspects in a certain hierarchical order. Holy Church allows and encourages us to let our hearts be especially drawn to one or several "aspects" of our God: to His Most Sacred Heart, His Blessed Mother, His Holy Face, His infancy, His poverty (as especially among Franciscans), His wisdom (as especially among Dominicans and Jesuits), His obedience (as especially among Benedictines), and so on. With us, however, the governing idea is that each one who adopts and lives a Rule of Life does so primarily as a Catholic who is uniting with all the others in the basic, necessary, and universal truths and requirements of the Faith.

It is for the glorification of the Father, for love of Our Blessed Lord and Savior Jesus Christ, and in the Holy Spirit that we pledge our whole heart, our whole soul, and our whole mind (cf. Mt 12:37) to the building up of the Mystical Body—the One, Holy, Catholic, and Apostolic Church—and the spread of His kingdom through our conversion, our true interior renewal and personal sanctification. This we can do—and can only do—with the powerful help of the Immaculate Virgin Mother of Our Lord and of His Church, with the intercession of St. Michael and all the angels, and under the protection of St. Joseph in union with St. Peter and St. Paul, our patron saints, and all the saints in Heaven.

To declare our purpose is one thing; to accomplish it is something very different indeed. In between, we must do those things which tend to the accomplishment of the purpose. And before that, we must learn what those things are. Therefore, we have to take our humble places in what St. Benedict called a "school of the Lord's service," where each will learn the answer to his question: "Lord, what would you have me do?"

We intend by this Rule of Life to learn and to do what the Holy Catholic Church in the Second Vatican Council has taught and exhorted us to do: to live the totality of the Gospel in the totality of our lives. Never before has the Church declared so clearly and emphatically that the vocation to holiness is universal, is a personal call of Christ to every single one of us to follow Him as closely and as constantly as His grace will enable us to do.

God's providence can surely be seen in the fact that His Church impressed upon all her children the universality of the vocation to holiness just at a moment in her history when enormous powers of evil were to be loosed against her. On April 4, 1967, less than two years after the close of the Second Vatican Council, the Sovereign Pontiff would have to speak of "this hour of darkness" in the Church; and five years later still (June 29, 1972), the Pope would say that "The smoke of Satan has entered the Temple of God."

We are living in an apocalyptic time of spiritual warfare "not against flesh and blood, but against principalities and powers, against the rulers of the world of this darkness, against the spirit of evil in high places" (Eph. 6:12). Merely human weapons are of no avail here; we can do battle only with the weapons of the saints, and especially by praying the Holy Rosary, which St. Padre Pio of Pietrelcina described as "the greatest weapon in the world against evil." With unprecedented urgency we are called to the defense of the Bride of Christ by being called to seek holiness. By this Rule of Life we respond to that call: "Here we are! Behold the servants and handmaids of the Lord!"

THE PRINCIPLES OF OUR LIFE: THE VIRTUES AND THE SACRAMENTS

Absolutely primordial to the life we profess is the gift of *supernatural faith*, the virtue infused in us by the grace of our Baptism. We exercise this virtue — we live this virtue — by freely committing our entire self to God, making the full submission of our intellect and will to God Who reveals, willingly assenting to the revelation given by Him (*Dei Verbum*, no. 5). We offer this "obedience of faith" (Rom 16:26) to God through His Church, for it is the Church's Magisterium (her teaching office) which alone authenticates for us the divine revelation, and keeps and nourishes us in the truth.

This Catholic Faith of ours, first given in Baptism, then ratified and "confirmed" in Confirmation, is essentially supernatural: it is beyond our unaided power to obtain or maintain. Yet *our cooperation is required.* It consists precisely in the exercise of our faith—"Lord, I believe; help my unbelief!" (Mk 9:23).

We can exercise our faith only to the extent that it is truly faith, and not sight (Jn 20:29). Therefore, this very time of darkness and confusion, when unbelief is so rampant in the world, is in God's providence an occasion for us to grow in pure faith. Surely there is reason to be thankful for this testing which slowly teaches us to live in the faith of the Son of God, Who loved us and gave Himself up for us (Gal 2:20). *His death is our life*—in faith. Without this faith we are nothing; but with it we can do all things (Mk 9:23).

St. Thomas Aquinas says it: "Faith is the foundation of our spiritual life" (*Summa Theologica*, III, q. 73, art. 3). St. Paul tells us: "Without faith it is impossible to please God" (Heb 11:6).

At first, we "know" it solely on the testimony of others. We find that what we know (in the darkness of faith) is lovable; and our love then urges us to know more. The more we come to know, the more we love. The more we love, the more we seek to know; and by this ascending alternation of loving and knowing we are on the way of being transformed in Christ. Therefore, it is undeniably God's will for us that we study our holy Faith with docile love, earnestness, and perseverance, holding fast always to the living Magisterium of the Church, the divinely willed channel and interpreter of the Faith.

Just as our spiritual life is the one ultimate foundation of our entire life, by giving it meaning and value, so the one rock-bottom foundation of our spiritual life is *faith.* Everything depends then on this primary task of ours: our knowing the truths of God, "professing them in our hearts, confessing them on our lips" (Rom 10:10), and growing in an ever deeper understanding of them. That is why, before all else, we Catholics are united in the Faith.

Following this gift of faith, and grounded in it, is the second infused virtue of Baptism and the Christian life: *hope.*

By virtue of it we can and must, as our father Abraham did, "hope against hope" (Rom 4:18). This hope is not "optimism" in any worldly or natural sense, any more than faith is "seeing" in any natural sense. It is rather the daring, trembling *desire* to possess what we grasp by faith: *God Himself in His infinite goodness*. It is the loving, trusting confidence in the infinite love and wondrous goodness of Jesus Who, for His part, will give us all the graces and helps we need for the total fulfillment of our desire.

Secondly, it is the serene, unshakable *confidence* in that same infinite goodness and power of God that that desire *will be* fulfilled. The fulfillment is hereafter, but the desire and the confidence are now. In His mercy we can be kept free from sin and protected from all anxiety as we wait in joyful hope for the coming of our Savior, Jesus Christ (cf. Ordinary of the Mass).

Hope is the virtue which enables us to accept peacefully the mysterious ways of God's providence, even if cares and trials threaten to overwhelm us, or we see the momentary triumph of evil, because we know that "His mercy endures forever" (Ps 135). In the humble and unshakeable confidence that we are infinitely loved by Jesus, that we have been ransomed and saved by His Most Precious Blood, the virtue of hope grows until we dare to say, "I can do all things in Him who strengthens me" (Phil 4:13).

As in the case of faith, so also here: we grow in hope by hoping. We must desire without limit, for God's goodness and beauty are limitless; and we must and can trust without limit, for God's power and mercy are limitless. If at times the world and our lives in it seem hopeless, in themselves they *are* hopeless. Only in God and His "sweet Word," Jesus, is there *any* hope—is there *all* our hope.

Faith and hope bring us to God; by means of them we are in the shadow of His wings (Ps 56:4; 90:4). But to make us one with Him, in "one Spirit" (1 Cor 6:17), can be done only by *charity*. To His revelation our response is the assent of faith, and to His promise our response is the desire and trust of hope. But what is revealed and promised is *Himself*; and our response to that is—and can only be—*love*, for God is Love (1 Jn 4:8). This love that is God will be the life of our seeing and possessing Him forever in Heaven, and it is the life of our faith and hope *now*.

Believing in Him and trusting Him now, we also love Him now. But how do we love Him now? We love Him as He loves us, for love first comes from Him (1 Jn 4:10). Yet, we of ourselves are so far from Him, so infinitely far, that we must start from our native nothingness. This is what Holy Scripture usually means when it speaks of "fear." Reverent awe is the proper stance of the creature before the Creator; that is why "the fear of the Lord is the beginning of wisdom" (Ps 110:1; Sir 1:14). It is only the beginning, however, for the wisdom rooted in reverence grows into its fulfillment; it flowers in love. Thus, we learn of His love through our awareness of our creatureliness, we grow in His love through our aspiring to His gifts, and we abide in His love through our mutual exchange of selves—which is our destiny forever.

This leads us to consider what we have done to make necessary such an outpouring of sacrificial love. Sheltered now in that love, we at last dare to look at ourselves with open eyes—we are shocked and appalled at what we see; an abyss of pride and lust and greed, a lifetime of self-seeking and ingratitude, a stony rejection of that divine love; and our hearts fill with compunction and repentance, begging forgiveness and healing. Then, at peace once more—it is a true peace, this time—in the arms of Our Father, we beg to be allowed to serve Him, we beg Him for what we need, knowing that we have no merits of our own by which we deserve God's gifts, but trusting in His fatherly love which allows us a share in the merits of His only begotten Son, our Model, Jesus Christ Crucified.

And what do we need, that we should beg Him for? We need *newness of life*. We need to die to ourselves, to be buried with Christ in Baptism that we may rise with Him. We must be prepared to suffer with Him if we are to enter with Him into His glory (cf. Lk 24:26). In our new life we need to be strengthened by His strength in Confirmation. But even at best we remain frail, our fallen nature continues to war against the new life of grace, and we turn from God to ourselves innumerable times—always again we need forgiveness and purification and strengthening in the Sacrament of Penance, or Reconciliation.

For such a destiny as living within the Sacred Heart of Jesus, our power to love must be purified and prepared. There must be a *metanoia*, a *conversio*, a turning away from all that could destroy or even in any way injure this divine gift, through a total turning to Him.

Penance, the reparation from past evil and the prevention of evil to come, must be, then, a constant element in our lives. So great is God's love for us that this is itself another gift to us: He has sacramentalized this penance of ours and made it His own (cf. 2 Cor 5:21). Through His Church He renews the grace of our baptism and confirmation by the Sacrament of Penance. And He does this in order to dispose us for His greatest gift of all—the Holy Eucharist.

THE CENTER OF OUR LIFE: THE ECCLESIAL-EUCHARIST MYSTERY

Beyond all gifts—the virtues and the sacraments of the divine life—is the giver Himself, from Whom descends every perfect gift (Js 1:17); and He crowns His gifts with the gift of Himself in the Holy Eucharist. In the Holy Eucharist we have the ultimate sacrament and the ultimate virtue: the efficacious sign of absolute love. Under the Eucharistic species of bread and wine, Jesus Christ, Son of the living God, gives Himself together with us to His Father in sacrifice, and gives Himself together with His Father to us in Holy Communion, in the unity of the one Holy Spirit.

Mass and Holy Communion constitute, therefore, in the simplest and most literal truth, the center of our life. Without the Eucharist we have no life in us (Jn 6:53); with it we have everything, for it is in itself "spirit and life" (Jn 6:63).

Here alone we have immediate contact with everything that is in any way destined for the eternal possession of God in Heaven. Here alone we can receive in its fullness, but according to our capacity to accept it, that charity by which we love God with all our heart and with the same heart love our neighbor as ourselves. In no other way is this possible but here, for by sharing in the one Bread, we become one Body, not only with Christ the head but with all His members. For only here do we have on earth the real body of Christ, both Eucharistic and Mystical: the one true Church by virtue of which, all the elect are in fact saved.

For the believing Catholic, the Church is not something following upon his belief—a mere convenience for promoting and sustaining pieties in like-minded "fellowship." Nor is it a mere "organization," no matter how sociologically necessary it may be. Rather, the Church is an *organism*, not merely formed by persons, but forming them—after the image of Christ, of Whom she is at once spouse and body.

The Catholic rightly calls the Church his Mother. Here is a relationship that, while essentially supernatural and mysterious, is also most elemental and "natural." Here is a loyalty beyond all other human loyalties, for here also is our one surest contact with the divine.

And what in turn is our one surest contact with the Church herself? In a Church that is meant by divine mandate to be co-extensive with the human race, and therefore literally catholic in the diversity of its facets, there is need for a sign: an actual representative and living embodiment of its identity and unity. That one sign is the office of Blessed Peter and the person occupying that office. "Where Peter is, there is the Church," just as "Where the Church is, there is Christ." That is why we as Catholics must affirm our unshakable loyalty to the Pope, and thus to the Church, and thus to Christ. That is why in the Supreme Pontiff—our "Holy Father"—the Catholic rightly sees the living sign of the One, Holy, Catholic, and Apostolic Church—the one family of God, wherein we are children who cherish and are cherished by our Mother and Father, and who in that household of faith and love grow up in the charity of the Eucharistic Christ.

This essential Eucharistic charity is therefore best expressed by our love for the holy Church. For if it is true that without the Eucharist there would be no Church, it is likewise true that without the Church there would be no Eucharist. This Church, holy and spotless as she is by virtue of Christ's presence in her, is also something less than holy by virtue of our presence in her. We must love and cherish her, then, in this weakness of hers—which is our weakness (*Lumen gentium*, no. 8).

Even here the ineffable love of God has anticipated us, for He has given us the perfect symbol of this love by which we must love His Church. That symbol is the Sacred Heart of Jesus. It was revealed to us in His death: the opened side of the crucified sleeping Christ and the issuing of the blood and water of His life.

In the undeviating tradition of the Fathers, this is *the* sign of the Church: the new Eve and mother of all the living; for this is the sacrament of all her sacraments and virtues, and the seal of the Holy Spirit. The historical reality of this sign was the physical death of Jesus on His cross, and the mystical continuation of that death through all the ages is the sufferings of His members in the Church. Indeed, the Ecclesial-Eucharistic Mystery is the Heart of Jesus—and therefore, the heart of our life.

THE INTERIORIZATION OF OUR LIFE: PRAYER

If it can be said that the whole life of the Church (and, therefore, our own life of grace), is a continuous ascending and descending the holy mountain of the Eucharist where He is enthroned on His cross, it can also be said that the whole activity of the Church (and of ourselves in union with her) is what we call *prayer*. For prayer is the very breath, the very breathing of that life. It is preeminently by prayer that we express our faith and hope, and by prayer that we grow in them. In its essence all our prayer is Eucharistic and Ecclesial, for it is to the voice of the Son that the Father's ear is always open: "If you ask the Father anything in My name, He will give it to you" (Jn 16:23). That is why every prayer of every Christian is offered "through Him, with Him, and in Him" (Ordinary of the Mass).

For everyone, then, his every prayer is centered on the Mass. The Church has made this real by making her *official* prayer a "liturgy of the hours," a ceaseless cycle of formal prayer setting off and surrounding each day's Mass. Not all the members of the Church are assigned actively to participate in this prayer, but all are invited to do so.

We must see in this invitation an opportunity of exceeding worth—to join with the clergy and the religious in singing the praises of God and the pleas of His people. Even when prayed alone and in silence, this sacred liturgy is of incalculable value, for it is both the spring and the reservoir of all our acts by which, in union with the whole Church, we raise our minds and hearts to God.

Besides this formal prayer, often called the "Divine Office" because it is our most official and God-like prayer, the Church offers her children from the inexhaustible treasury of her tradition many other kinds of formal prayer, hallowed by her saints and sanctioned by her authority. The most ready examples of such prayer are the Benediction of the Blessed Sacrament (that perfect little reminder of Mass and Holy Communion), the Rosary (that perfect amalgam of meditation and petition, of the mental and the vocal), the Stations of the Cross, the Angelus, and our "grace" at meals. The variety and unity of these and all her formulated prayers are eminently Catholic—as Catholic, indeed, as the balance with which she safeguards and promotes their usage.

These prayers in the Church's treasury are wonderfully adaptable: they belong to each of us exclusively, and they belong to all. In fact, our praying together adds more than the dimension of mere numbers. We have Our Lord's promise that He will be in our midst (Mt 18:20). Our parishes are at their best when we pray as a parish. And even more truly, putting our prayer and our families together can be the very perfection of our prayer.

But, before we "say our prayers," whether with others or alone, there is the indispensable *preparation* enjoined by Our Lord Himself: "When you pray, go into your room and shut the door" (Mt 6:6). This means *silence*—interior silence; and in a noisy world such silence must be carefully sought.

We must be clear about what silence is. It is not nothing, a mere absence. It is adoring and listening; it is alive, like the silence of a candle flame. "You have died," says the Apostle, "and your life is hidden with Christ in God" (Col 3:3–4). Idle conversation, idle diversion—much more than our souls need, indeed much more than our souls can stand—must be removed if we are ever really to pray.

Preparation for prayer demands more, however, than mere removals. We must not only eliminate the drafts impeding our candle; we must fuel the flame. This means, first and most importantly, *reading*: that *lectio divina* which in the Patristic tradition is so integral to prayer that it is hard to say where the reading leaves off and the prayer begins.

Among all possible readings, Holy Scripture holds the first place, for it gives us the very words of God Himself. And the heart of Holy Scripture is in the Gospels, for there we meet the one living Word of God, the Word Incarnate. It is this living Word that all the saints have pondered, and prayed to, and written about (Lk 2:19, 51; 10:40–42). And as we in turn ponder their words, they, like stepping stones, lead us back to the living Word, so that we, making that Word our own, can then truly pray.

Now prayer thus described—the authentic Catholic prayer of the Scripture and the Tradition—in its preparation and in its exercise does not admit of "short cuts." The one recourse—and it is an uncomfortable word in this age of comfort—is *discipline*. Where a man's treasure is, there will his heart be also (Mt 6:21). And where a man's heart is, there he finds time, there he listens to nothing else. We must decide with firmest resolve not only to extend the amount of time we set aside for communion with God, but also to intensify the earnestness with which we seek His face and listen to His voice.

The great obstacle always seems to be lack of time: "I am a busy lay-person." But it is a common experience of those who have tried it that more time for prayer actually makes our daily work easier. Through God's grace we are calmer and more recollected, and our work is more expeditiously performed.

The exercise of prayer must be constant with us—as constant as our breathing. Our Lord has told us that we must pray always (Lk 18:1), and especially at the very times we find it most difficult to do so (Lk 22:40). That is why we need discipline.

If we are commanded to shut out the world while at prayer, and if we are commanded to pray always, then we must, by discipline, fashion an "interior enclosure" in which our souls may dwell even when we are sent out into the world about our Father's business.

We learn to pray by praying. It can become habitual with us, just as it was habitual with the saints. But, just as with the saints, we must see ourselves always as beginners. Contemplation, which is the highest kind of prayer—since it anticipates the very life of Heaven—is a gift we should desire, but only in order thereby to love God the more. For only charity gives us the Giver Himself; He is the gift beyond all gifts, even the gift of prayer. Thus, we are beginners and will always be such in this life. And this is as it should be, since only as children can we enter the kingdom of Heaven (Mt 18:3).

THE EXTERIORIZATION OF OUR LIFE: WORK

Prayer is the most important of all the "good works" without which our faith is dead (Jas 2:20). Indeed, in a certain sense, it is the only "good work," for without it nothing reaches God. In the same sense, our whole life must be prayer (1 Thess 5:16). Yet, there is the obvious distinction between prayer that is formally such, and prayer that is not. Formal prayer—whether "formulated" liturgically or otherwise, or "unformulated" in strict solitude or otherwise—can only be part of our total lives; but it must be the most important part, since it "informs" the whole and makes that whole an *informal* prayer by which whatever we do, we do for the glory of God (1 Cor 10:31).

All our prayer should receive a special ardor from our longing for the welfare and salvation of our neighbor; and all our apostolic labors should be infused and glowing with our total love of God.

Among all these works that compose the pattern of our earthly lives, there are two which from Holy Scripture and the earliest traditions of the Church actually have been put alongside formal prayer as the good works *par excellence*: fasting and almsgiving.

In its formal sense, fasting is still, however minimally, a mandatory matter. But informally it can be co-extensive with our lives, just as informal prayer is. Fasting means *mortification* or self-denial: the turning from and dying to self, in order to turn to and live to God.

Similarly, almsgiving in its informal sense serves as the equivalent of all the so-called works of mercy: those ministries of love to our neighbor, which test the efficaciousness of our love for God.

Prayer, fasting, almsgiving—turning to God, from self, through the neighbor: here is the work that we are here on earth to do. It is the work of Christ and His holy Church; it is what He came to do, and what He commissioned His Apostles to do after Him until the end of time. The apostolate is essentially this being sent by Christ: to witness His truth and minister His mercy to all mankind—and beginning with those of our household, and of the household of the Faith (Gal 6:10). This is what we have been called to do, not as an "extra" to our achieving salvation but as essential to it; we can ourselves be saved no other way (Mt 25:40, 45).

The universal call to holiness is, therefore, strictly the same as the universal call to the apostolate. They are but one call, and this call is to all. We take our part, then, both by duty and by right, in the apostolic work of the Church. This is our vocation, in both its most immediate and its most far-reaching sense. Everything else we do, for earning a livelihood or for anything else, is but an "avocation"—a desirable or even an urgent but still only a negotiable adjunct to the "one thing necessary" (Lk 10:42).

There are two distinct areas of apostolic work in which we of the laity are to be engaged. The first is the area proper to the laity, that area so reserved to them, in fact, that if they do not work it, it will not be worked at all. This area is best called simply "the world"—the *saeculum* created originally as "very good" (Gen 1:31), but then mysteriously infected by the "Mystery of Iniquity" (2 Thess 2:7). This world, which is both around us and within us, must be *redeemed* in all its extent of time and space.

The redemption effected by Christ must be applied by *our* extending it by our work to that segment of time and space that is *our* world. We extend it, first of all, by our working simply in terms of justice: our giving to all—our individual neighbor, our employer or employee, our government at whatever level, our associations of whatever kind—that which by the law of nature and of nature's God is their due. Then, faithful to the way in which Christ effected the whole world's redemption, we redeem our little world by going beyond strict justice; we emulate His mercy. Our norm is no longer the neighbor's due, loving him as we love ourselves, but rather Christ's "due": loving the neighbor as Christ loves him—and us.

The second area of the laity's work is that of our cooperation with the clergy in the area proper to them—the sacred witness and ministry of the Gospel. The *sacrum* that is preached in the word of God and administered in the sacraments is essentially confided to the bishops, priests, and deacons of the Church; for on them alone has been conferred Christ's own power to sanctify: the Sacrament of Holy Orders.

Yet the laity can *cooperate* in the exercise of this sacred power. By virtue of the Sacraments of Baptism and Confirmation, the laity also has its own proper priestly function (1 Peter 2:9)—by witnessing to and exercising its faith and charity according to the state of life to which God has called each one, whether in the married or in the single life. We are called to spread the Faith, to evangelize.

To perform this sacred function, we laity must prepare ourselves by diligently studying the truths of our Faith. We should also prepare worthy candidates for Holy Orders and the religious life from our own families and fellow parishioners—young people trained in the "magisterium" and pastoral discipline of their own homes.

The two areas of the world and the Church—of the profane and the sacred, of the natural and the supernatural—are indeed distinct but never separated. They are in fact *inseparable*, as inseparable (in a sense) as the bond of that institution which God from the beginning willed for the unity and continuity of His entire creation. That bond is marriage, and that institution is the family. Here, then, is a vocation that is specifically a lay vocation. It marks the culminating activity and grace of a lay person as such, and places each man and woman in the sacramental order. The family is the "domestic Church." All holiness for the married person begins—and ends—in the home.

THE CONSUMMATION OF OUR LIFE: THE PASCHAL MYSTERY AND THE COMMUNION OF SAINTS

In the course of a lifetime of prayer and work we will experience again and again the inadequacy, the incompleteness, even the failure of our best efforts. All the saints have experienced it before us; and we shall not escape it in our days, when the sheer magnitude of evil to be overcome and the need for goodness and truth have never been greater.

We should never allow ourselves to be the least bit discouraged by this experience. First of all, our "best efforts" are often not all they should be. Secondly, even the best efforts sometimes fail of their goal. Thirdly, it often happens that the feeling is only a disguise for our vexation that our efforts receive neither thanks nor even recognition (Lk 17:9–10).

But this real failure of ours is more than matched by Christ's own "failure"—as the world measures things. He ultimately fulfilled His task—the will of His Father and the salvation of the world—not by His words and works, but by

His sufferings and death. He was "fulfilled" only in His failure. And He clearly told us that we must follow Him in this: His Way of the Cross (Mt 16:24).

The Cross of Christ will always be what it has always been: the Sign of Contradiction (Lk 2:34), the supreme paradox of the Gospel. Only by losing one's life will one keep it, only by falling into the ground and dying will the seed become more than a seed (Jn 12:24–25). This losing, this dying is no mere metaphor; it is painfully, desperately real. The saints did not "enjoy" their sufferings, neither did Our Lord. His prayer in Gethsemane (Mt 26:39) has become the prayer of His Church. By virtue of that prayer and the power of His Passion, we can imitate the saints in what is most imitable in them—*their littleness*. We too can glory in our infirmities (2 Cor 12:10), for only then will Christ the Savior—the Crucified—become manifest in us.

The final manifestation of Christ in us, His full identification with us, can be achieved only by our death. The seal of His Cross is upon us from the beginning: from our baptism and all the sacraments, including now (if God's providence so wills) the last Anointing of the Sick and the Holy Viaticum. But only in death will *mortification*—the turning from self—be completed; so too only then will the *vivification* become a total reality—becoming one with the Living God.

We anticipate that all-important moment of our death with every Mass and Holy Communion, and even with every Hail Mary. In so doing, we prepare the Pasch—our entrance into the ultimate Mystery of Christ and the innermost chamber of His Sacred Heart.

The Heart of Jesus, though still wounded, is now in glory. Indeed, His wounds are the glory of the risen Christ. Standing as though slain (Apoc 5:6), Christ is both Priest and Victim before His Father; and His Holy Spirit now fills the world, forming and vivifying the body of which Christ is the head. Yesterday and today and forever the risen Lord (Heb 13:5), Jesus is indeed exalted and draws all things to Himself (Jn 12:32).

Just as our present sufferings are His past sufferings, so His present glory is our future glory. Christ "lifted up" in His Crucifixion and in His Ascension, ourselves dying and glorying in our death: the two phases of the Paschal Mystery are as truly one as the man Jesus is one with His Father and we are one with Him. The Paschal Mystery is thus the summation of the Gospel—and our Rule of Life.

By the power of his Spirit, the Christ of the Paschal Mystery fills all creation (Mt 28:18; Eph 4:10; Phil 2:10). This *Christus Totus* is the "Jesus of history" together with all the scattered children He has gathered (Jn 11:52) and made His brethren (Jn 20:17). By faith and baptism, we have been incorporated into Him, to form His Body; by charity and the Holy Eucharist this one body lives in one Spirit.

There are those who are already Blessed in the "vision of peace"—the saints in Heaven. And there are those who are still in purgation, although assured of salvation—the saints in Purgatory. And finally, there are ourselves, in the grace of the pilgrim and militant Church—the saints on earth. We will more surely reach the destination of the cross we carry if we remember those who have gone before us and who now watch over us as a cloud of witnesses (Heb 12:1).

Among all those blessed ones who watch over us, one is preeminent—the glorious and Immaculate Virgin Mary. As both virgin and mother, and as both redeemed and co-redeeming, Our Lady is the perfect prototype of the Holy Church. She is the one actual consummation of God's creative and redemptive plan. With wonder we echo the proclamation of the Holy Father in the Second Vatican Council: "Mary is Mother of the Church." She is Mother of God, Mother of the total Christ, Mother of *me*. To her Immaculate Heart we commend the past and the present of our lives, and the future as envisioned by this Rule of Life. This commendation is absolute, for we know that it is the surest way to enter the Sacred Heart of Jesus, Who is our Alpha and Omega, *our very All*.

REFLECTIONS FROM THE SAINTS

"Yes, my heart's dear one, Jesus is here with His Cross. Since you are one of His favorites, He wants to make you into His likeness; why be afraid that you will not have the strength to carry this cross without a struggle? On the way to Calvary, Jesus did indeed fall three times and you, poor little child, would like to be different from your Spouse, would rather not fall a hundred times if necessary to prove your love to Him by getting back up with even more strength than before your fall!" —ST. THÉRÈSE OF LISIEUX

"If you suffer with Him, you will reign with Him. If you cry with Him, you will have joy with Him. If you die with Him on the Cross of Tribulation, you will possess the eternal dwelling place in the splendor of the saints. And your name, written in the Book of Life, will be glorious among men." —ST. CLARE OF ASSISI

"Confession heals, confession justifies, confession grants pardon of sin. All hope consists in confession. In confession there is a chance for mercy. Believe it firmly, do not doubt, do not hesitate, never despair of the mercy of God." —ST. ISIDORE OF SEVILLE

"You don't know how to pray? Put yourself in the presence of God, and as soon as you have said, 'Lord, I don't know how to pray!' you can be sure you've already begun." —ST. JOSEMARIA ESCRIVA

"The life of a Christian is nothing but a perpetual struggle against self; there is no flowering of the soul to the beauty of its perfection except at the price of pain." —ST. PADRE PIO

"Cast yourself into the arms of God and be very sure that if He wants anything of you, He will fit you for the work and give you strength." —ST. PHILIP NERI

CHAPTER ELEVEN

A PERSONAL RULE OF LIFE FOR OUR JOURNEY INTO THE SACRED HEART OF JESUS

> *"I am the vine; you are the branches. Whoever remains in me, with me in him, bears fruit in plenty; for cut off from me you can do nothing. Anyone who does not remain in me is like a branch that has been thrown away—he withers.... If you remain in me and my words remain in you, you may ask what you will and you shall get it" (Jn 15:5–7).*

IF THERE IS A NEED FOR SOMETHING "SPECIFIC" beyond our simple and total commitment to Catholic spirituality as derived from Tradition and enunciated by the Second Vatican Council, the particular cachet or hallmark of Catholic spirituality—namely, that which should identify it and summarize its Rule of Life—would be the following formulation:

> The Catholic's Rule of Life has as the criterion of both its authenticity and its efficacity *a three-fold devotion*: to the Holy Eucharist, to our Lady, the Blessed Mother, and to the Vicar of Christ.

It is no accident that historically these three realities, as inter-related mediations of the one core mystery and reality of the Incarnation, have invariably evoked the same response among Christian people: either all three are revered and loved, or all three are (sooner or later) downgraded and ignored. Catholics, therefore, must be unequivocally *Petrine, Marian, and Eucharistic*. For so is the Catholic Church, having as she has, the mind of Christ.

The discussion which follows "spells out" the foregoing Rule of Life. Both its specificity and its adaptability should indicate with sufficient clarity its relationship to our efforts to live within the Sacred Heart of Jesus. This Rule is meant for those who wish to go beyond the minimum set by the Church for remaining in the state of grace; yet in its aspiring toward that maximum which is ever beyond us, it is hopefully, humbly, realistically flexible.

This little School of the Lord's Service has three traditional levels: first, second, and third, for we must all know that no matter how long we may live or how hard we may try or what "successes" we may think we have had here or there, we will always remain small children in the sight of God. When He commands us to become as little children, He is only asking us to recognize humbly that that is what we are, and to rejoice.

PRAENOTANDA

This schedule follows a time-tested tradition when it "measures" growth in the pursuit of holiness by certain quantitative norms. It is faithful to the same tradition when it sets "levels" to these norms.

It relates these quantitative norms ("how much") to the substance itself ("what"), which it summarizes under seven headings of agenda for each level.

AGENDA OF THE FIRST LEVEL

Who may take the first step along this walk to be united within the Sacred Heart of Jesus? The requirements are that you want to begin the journey because you recognize that you need order, discipline, companionship, and help along the road to eternal life with God. You realize that you need the help of Holy Mother Church, Our Lord Jesus, our Mother Mary, the saints, and fellow Catholics along the way.

The First Level requires that I will endeavor to fulfill the following, *if at all possible*:

1. *Mass and Holy Communion*
   At least one day, besides Sunday, each week.
2. *Confession*
   At least once each month.
3. *Prayer/Reading*
   At least one half-hour each day (apart from Mass, which should always be given priority over every other form of prayer), including at least one decade of the Rosary. Also, adopting the habit of frequent aspirations, e.g., invoking the Holy Name of Jesus or praying "Jesus, I place all my trust in you." (For family members, this agendum should take into account the training of young children in prayer.)
4. *Mortification*
   At least one explicit act of self-denial each day (apart from abstinence from meat each Friday), e.g., curtailing the time for television and browsing on the Internet, giving up dessert or a favorite food or drink, giving up your time for relaxation by offering to help someone with a time-consuming chore.
5. *Works of Mercy*
   Witnessing to and teaching the Faith where possible and appropriate, beginning in the home. Regular contribution to some specific work of charity, such as visiting the sick or the elderly in nursing homes, assisting with jail ministries, driving the elderly, disabled or cancer patients to appointments, and volunteering to work with such charitable organizations as Meals on Wheels.
6. *Apostolic Action*
   This can include membership in various third orders such as the Franciscans, Carmelites and Dominicans, and participating in their apostolates, such as operating food pantries in parishes, or individual apostolates, including serving as catechists in parishes or volunteering with the Society of St. Vincent de Paul.
7. *Guidance*
   Annual retreat of at least one weekend and longer if possible.

Do these small steps as your journey begins seem difficult or even impossible to take? Where are you going to find the time? There is a big problem in the lives of most of us today: the *apparent shortage of time*. Here we must say that before relying upon that excuse, we ought to make sure that it is genuine — we ought to examine with honesty and care our habitual use of this precious gift of time. If we were to keep a detailed record over a typical week, most of us would be astonished to see how easily and how much we fritter time away — time which belongs not to us but to God, Who entrusts it to us, as stewards, that we may win through to everlasting life by learning to know, love, and serve Him in this life.

There may perhaps be persons who, for one reason or another, cannot give sixty or even thirty minutes consecutively each day to prayer; but they are rare in reality. Most of us will find that we spend considerably more time than that each day in pampering our bodies, attending to that coffee break with perhaps a few snacks in between, watching TV, mindlessly scrolling the Internet, randomly reading newspapers, magazines, advertisements and the back of cereal boxes, shopping with no clear or necessary object in view — and many other pastimes.

This Rule assumes two truths: that it does often seem hard to find time; and that a little extra genuine effort will almost always disclose that there is more of it available than we had supposed.

The minimal requirements of the First Level of the Rule of Life are just that: *minimal*, without which it would be fanciful to call oneself anything more than a minimal Catholic. But this Rule is addressed to those who know that they must be more than a minimal Catholic — to men and women who believe that God has called them to seek their holiness and to fulfill their apostolate that He has willed for them.

Holiness means identification with God. That is why Jesus Christ alone can be called the Holy One. For us, holiness means union with the Holy One to the full extent of our limited capacities; and that means not just seeking Him in prayer but also imitating Him Who was also given a work to do, and Who accomplished it (cf. Jn 17:4). The way to that union is by a total, eager, loving docility to the will of the Father, the teachings of the Son, and the promptings of the

Holy Spirit, in every event of every day. By such docility we say our own personal *Fiat!* to a birth of Christ in our hearts and souls.

It is the will of God that His Son be incarnate; it is His will that each of us try to imitate the Blessed Virgin and Mother of the Word, each opening his heart to the Holy Spirit so that Christ may live in it. The total Christ cannot live in my small heart—but my small heart can be totally filled with Christ. And it *must* be so filled. We live in a world which is turned away from God, a world which is wounded and fragmented. Consequently, there is an urgent need for holiness which alone converts, heals, and unifies. That is why union with Christ and hopefully dwelling within His Sacred Heart is indispensable for any good work.

We have seen that the call to holiness and the call to the apostolate constitute one call, addressed to each of us—that the general vocation of the laity is a mixed vocation. Therefore, it is not enough that the Rule of Life prescribes an irreducible minimum of prayer; it must also provide for the fundamentals of our apostolate. There are evidently many sorts and conditions of laymen and women: those who have been placed by God in the married state, those who have been placed in the single state, the old, the sick, and young people.

For all of us, without exception, it is necessary to plan the use of God's gifts, and to put our plans into practice. We who are grown up may no longer indulge that "refreshing obliviousness" which we see in children as they flit at random from one activity to another. The spontaneity of our hearts must express itself in a sanctioned activity. Everything must be done in considered and joyful obedience.

The necessary planning is made both easier and more necessary by the fact that, for each individual, the daily occupations tend to fall into recurring categories, such as: eating, sleeping, prayer, work, recreation, conversation, reading, housework, and practicing charity. For married persons with children, there is the care of the family. For others, both single and married, it may be necessary to care for aging parents, family members, and often neighbors or friends. And among all the activities, there are the daily interruptions and annoyances, such as doctor appointments, becoming sick with things like the flu, traffic troubles while commuting back and forth to work, vehicles breaking down, etc. The list is endless, it seems.

On the other hand, planning a daily schedule for our Rule of Life is made more difficult by the fact that we forget about obedience, and "let ourselves go," doing whatever draws us at a given moment. St. Paul urges us to behave quite otherwise: "All whatsoever you do in word or in work, do all in the name of Jesus Christ, giving thanks to God the Father by Him" (Col 3:17).

If we block out a typical day's schedule of sixteen hours, from awaking to retiring for the day, we often will find that we have in a twenty-four-hour day about one to two hours that are unassigned to any particular tasks, even after devoting an hour to prayer. What are we going to do with these extra unassigned hours? Holiness has been said to be the perfect fulfilling of our duties in the state of life in which God has placed us. One quality which is common to every state of life is that the day is twenty-four hours long. If we are going to achieve holiness at all, we all have to do it within that time frame.

Since the schedule assumes that a person is awake and active sixteen hours every day, if, two times every hour, we stop for one minute, recollect ourselves into the loving presence of God (on our knees if possible), and in conscious union with the Holy Mass being celebrated somewhere at this moment, say: "Together with the Sacrifice of Jesus, I offer myself as a servant of the Lord; Christ, be merciful to me, a sinner!"—how pleasing that would be to God, and how refreshing and nourishing to our souls! And two minutes each hour, for sixteen hours, comes to more than half an hour a day. Can anyone say he has not time?

We are called to prepare ourselves for His service, and then to serve Him.

AGENDA OF THE SECOND LEVEL

To go on to the Second Level, more is required. We must be eager to go on because the love of Christ urges us to continue in the path to which His special mercy has led us. And this longing makes us recognize more clearly how poor we are and how much help we need, so that we resolve, with God's grace and within the possibilities which His providence allows, to move further along in our journey to live within the Sacred Heart of Jesus.

In addition to those seven steps of the First Level, I will endeavor to fulfill the following, *if at all possible*:

1. *Mass and Holy Communion*

At least three weekdays each week.

2. *Confession*

At least once each month, and examination of conscience once each day.

3. *Prayer/Reading*

At least three quarters of an hour each day, including five decades of the Rosary, and the Benedictus and the Magnificat from the Liturgy of the Hours. (This reading should keep in mind the priority of Sacred Scripture.) A Holy Hour once each month either in an Adoration Chapel if one is available or in front of the Tabernacle in a quiet church.

4. *Mortification*

At least one explicit act of self-denial each day (apart from abstinence from meat and dessert twice each week) and other explicit denials of pleasurable activities, such as further curtailing of television and scrolling the Internet, and similar diversions.

5. *Works of Mercy*

Contribution to works of charity cumulatively equivalent to tithing.

6. *Apostolic Action*

Active membership in third orders or participation in other activities as described in the First Level, including such activities as membership in the Knights of Columbus, leading parish Rosaries before or after Mass, Adoration Societies, pro-life ministry, sacristan, choir, and other activities in the parish or diocese.

7. *Guidance*

Annual retreat, days of recollection, and a regular confessor. If at all possible, ask the regular confessor to provide spiritual advice to help you discover and overcome vices and failings in order to develop the virtues.

AGENDA OF THE THIRD LEVEL

Most of our emphasis has been on the "going in" to be taught and nourished and to grow in love. But love, if it is genuine and if it is to continue to grow, must express itself in deeds. We must, all along, seriously take up our mission to "go out," to bring the Good News to the world around us in an active apostolate of service and evangelization.

Finally now, while living in the midst of the world as laymen and women, we are carrying the burden of the world's work (raising families in the love of God, filling the ranks of the professions, assuming the responsibilities of government, serving in the military, working in blue collar and service jobs, and contributing to the well-being of others). But we want above all and before all to give all our hearts and souls and strength to the service of God, His Church, and His children. This will entail a still deeper, more conscious commitment to growth in the spiritual life. It will also mean a greater generosity in the works of mercy—especially the spiritual works.

Everyone taking up this task to proceed to the Third Level will know, with ever greater certainty, that they cannot "go it alone." They will know, with ever greater conviction, that without Christ they can do nothing, and so they will always be praying, always "going in" to the fountains of living water.

In addition to those steps of the First and Second Levels, I will endeavor to fulfill the following, *if at all possible*:

1. *Mass and Holy Communion*

Every day unless sick, poor weather prevents safe driving, or there is no access to Mass while on vacation or traveling. I will see Holy Mass and Holy Communion as the *source, center and goal of all my actions* each day.

2. *Confession*

Once each week, with examination of conscience twice each day (noon and bedtime).

3. *Prayer/Reading*
At least one and a half hours each day, including five decades of the Rosary and Lauds or Vespers from the Liturgy of the Hours, and a Holy Hour each month. (This reading should expand to include Fathers of the Church, writings of the Magisterium, the Catechism of the Catholic Church, and lives of the saints, as well as spiritual and devotional books.)

4. *Mortification*
At least one explicit act of self-denial each day (apart from abstinence from meat and dessert twice each week and on an additional day in Advent and Lent).

5. *Works of Mercy*
Contribution to works of charity cumulatively equivalent to tithing, teaching the faith in the home and community, plus one visit to a hospital, nursing home, or jail, or pro-life work each month according to one's state in life.

6. *Apostolic Action*
Participation in third order activities as described in the First Level or greater use of one's talent in evangelization through the spoken and written word. This can include active participation in parish or diocesan youth ministries, assisting with jail ministries, serving in soup kitchens and shelters for the homeless, and writing spiritual articles for various publications such as Catholic magazines, newspapers, and Internet sites.

7. *Guidance*
Annual retreat of longer duration than a weekend (if possible), plus a day of recollection each quarter; regular confessor/spiritual director. In a sanctioned docility to the spiritual adviser, seek to live the spirit of the evangelical counsels by a constant effort to live according to the Beatitudes. Let persons with property remember that those are blessed who are poor in spirit and that there must be generous sharing with the poor. Let all bear in mind that only the pure in heart shall see God. And let those in any positions of authority strive to learn from Him Who is meek and humble of heart and Who became obedient, even unto the death of the Cross.

There are days of special devotion (apart from Sundays and holy days of obligation) at which we should assist at Mass and receive Holy Communion:

St. Peter's Chair	February 22
St. Joseph	March 19
Annunciation of the Lord	March 25
Sacred Heart of Jesus	Friday after Corpus Christi Sunday
Immaculate Heart of Mary	Saturday after Sacred Heart of Jesus
Sts. Peter and Paul	June 29
Exaltation of the Holy Cross	September 14

In addition, we should have special devotions on the feast days of our patron saints (Baptismal and Confirmation). For third order members, we should attend Mass, offer special prayers such as litanies, and read short biographies on the feast days of our order's founders and patron saints. It is also helpful to begin a novena leading up to the feast days of our order's saints.

It is beneficial to seek out other members in the parish or third order (if one belongs) with whom it may be possible to form a little group or community of common prayer and mutual help.

If we start and persevere along this path to living within the Sacred Heart of Jesus, we can be certain that He Who has given us the grace to begin will also give us all we need to win through to victory. As a pledge of this, we have the following words of the Second Vatican Council, with which we conclude our discussion of this Rule of Life. The words are taken from sections 33 and 34 of the Dogmatic Constitution on the Church, *Lumen gentium*:

> The apostolate of the laity is a sharing in the salvific mission of the Church.... [T]he supreme and eternal priest, Christ Jesus, vivifies them with His spirit and ceaselessly impels them to accomplish every good and perfect work.... Hence the laity, dedicated as they are to Christ and anointed by the Holy Spirit, are marvelously called and prepared so that even richer fruits of the Spirit may be produced in them. For all their works, prayers, and apostolic undertakings, family and married life, daily work, relaxation of mind and body, if they are accomplished in the Spirit—indeed even the hardships of life if patiently borne—all these become spiritual sacrifices acceptable to God through Jesus Christ (cf. Pet 2:5). In the celebration of the Eucharist these may

most fittingly be offered to the Father along with the Body of the Lord. *And so, worshipping everywhere by their holy actions, the laity consecrate the world itself to God.*

REFLECTIONS FROM THE SAINTS

"Lord, teach me to be generous. Teach me to serve you as you deserve; to give and not to count the cost; to fight, and not to heed the wounds; to toil, and not to seek for rest; to labor and not to ask for reward, except that of knowing that we are doing your will." —ST. IGNATIUS OF LOYOLA

"I will attempt day by day to break my will into pieces. I want to do God's Holy Will, not my own." —ST. GABRIEL POSSENTI

"Every pious desire, every good thought, every charitable work inspired by the love of Jesus, contributes to the perfection of the whole body of the faithful. A person who does nothing more than lovingly pray to God for his brethren participates in the great work of saving souls." —BL. ANNE CATHERINE EMMERICH

"What does love look like? It has the hands to help others. It has the feet to hasten to the poor and needy. It has eyes to see misery and want. It has the ears to hear the sighs and sorrows of men. That is what love looks like." —ST. AUGUSTINE

"When the Sisters are exhausted, up to their eyes in work, when all seems to go awry, they spend an hour in prayer before the Blessed Sacrament. This practice has never failed to bear fruit: they experience peace and strength." —ST. THERESA OF CALCUTTA

"True penance consists in regretting without ceasing the faults of the past, and in firmly resolving to never again commit that which is so deplorable." —ST. BERNARD OF CLAIRVAUX

FOR PRAYER AND GUIDANCE ON THE PATHWAY TO THE SACRED HEART OF JESUS

"What does Jesus Christ do in the Eucharist? It is God Who, as our Savior, offers Himself each day for us to His Father's justice. If you are in difficulties and sorrows, He will comfort and relieve you. If you are sick, He will either cure you or give you strength to suffer so as to merit Heaven. If the devil, the world, and the flesh are making war upon you, He will give you the weapons with which to fight, to resist, and to win victory. If you are poor, He will enrich you with all sorts of riches for time and eternity. Let us open the door of His Sacred and adorable Heart and be wrapped about for an instant by the flames of His love, and we shall see what a God who loves us can do. O my God, who shall be able to comprehend?" —ST. JOHN VIANNEY

ACT OF CONSECRATION TO THE SACRED HEART OF JESUS

By St. Margaret Mary Alacoque

O Sacred Heart of Jesus, to Thee I consecrate and offer up my person and my life, my actions, trials, and sufferings, that my entire being may henceforth only be employed in loving, honoring and glorifying Thee. This is my irrevocable will, to belong entirely to Thee, and to do all for Thy love, renouncing with my whole heart all that can displease Thee.

I take Thee, O Sacred Heart, for the sole object of my love, the protection of my life, the pledge of my salvation, the remedy of my frailty and inconstancy, the reparation for all the defects of my life, and my secure refuge at the hour of my death. Be Thou, O Most Merciful Heart, my justification before God Thy Father, and screen me from His anger which I have so justly merited. I fear all from my own weakness and malice, but placing my entire confidence in Thee, O Heart of Love, I hope all from Thine infinite Goodness.

Annihilate in me all that can displease or resist Thee. Imprint Thy pure love so deeply in my heart that I may never forget Thee or be separated from Thee. I beseech Thee, through Thine infinite Goodness, grant that my name be engraved upon Thy Heart, for in this I place all my happiness and all my glory, to live and to die as one of Thy devoted servants.

CHAPLET OF THE HOLY FACE OF JESUS

[*Note*: This devotion is intended to make reparation for the sins of blasphemy committed against Our Lord's Holy Face through His five senses. It is prayed to thwart the enemies of God.]

O God, come to my assistance; O Lord make haste to help me.

Glory be to the Father, and to the Son, and to the Holy Spirit. As it was in the beginning, is now, and ever shall be, world without end. Amen.

In honor of the sense of TOUCH of Jesus. My Jesus Mercy! *Glory be...*

Arise, O Lord! And let Thy enemies be scattered, and let them that hate Thee flee from before Thy Face. (Pray six times.)

In honor of the sense of HEARING of Jesus. My Jesus Mercy! *Glory be...*

Arise, O Lord! And let Thy enemies be scattered, and let them that hate Thee flee from before Thy Face. (Pray six times.)

In honor of the sense of SIGHT of Jesus. My Jesus Mercy! *Glory be...*

Arise, O Lord! And let Thy enemies be scattered, and let them that hate Thee flee from before Thy Face. (Pray six times.)

In honor of the sense of SMELL of Jesus. My Jesus Mercy! *Glory be...*

Arise, O Lord! And let Thy enemies be scattered, and let them that hate Thee flee from before Thy Face. (Pray six times.)

In honor of the sense of TASTE of Jesus. My Jesus Mercy! *Glory be...*

Arise, O Lord! And let Thy enemies be scattered, and let them that hate Thee flee from before Thy Face. (Pray six times.)

In honor of the three years of Our Lord's public ministry on earth. My Jesus Mercy! *Glory be...*

Arise, O Lord! And let Thy enemies be scattered, and let them that hate Thee flee from before Thy Face. (Pray three times.)
God, our Protector look on us and look on the Face of Thy Christ. Amen.

CONSECRATION TO THE PRECIOUS BLOOD OF JESUS

Conscious, merciful Savior, of my nothingness and of Thy sublimity, I cast myself at Thy feet and thank Thee for the many proofs of Thy grace shown unto me, Thy ungrateful creature. I thank Thee especially for delivering me by Thy Precious Blood from the destructive power of Satan.

In the presence of my dear Mother Mary, my guardian angel, my patron saint, and of the whole company of Heaven, I dedicate myself voluntarily with a sincere heart, O dearest Jesus, to Thy Precious Blood, by which Thou hast redeemed the world from sin, death and Hell.

I promise Thee, with the help of Thy grace and to the utmost of my strength, to stir up and foster devotion to Thy Precious Blood, the price of our redemption, so that Thy adorable Blood may be honored and glorified by all. In this way, I wish to make reparation for my disloyalty towards Thy Precious Blood of love, and to make satisfaction to Thee for the many profanations which men commit against that precious price of their salvation.

O would that my own sins, my coldness, and all the acts of disrespect I have ever committed against Thee, O Holy Precious Blood, could be undone.

Behold, O dearest Jesus, I offer to Thee the love, honor, and adoration which Thy most Holy Mother, Thy faithful disciples, and all the saints have offered to Thy Precious Blood. I ask Thee to forget my earlier faithlessness and coldness, and to forgive all who offend Thee.

Sprinkle me, O Divine Saviour, and all men, with Thy Precious Blood, so that we, O Crucified Love, may love Thee from now on with all our hearts, and worthily honor the price of our salvation. Amen.

CONSECRATION TO JESUS IN THE MOST HOLY EUCHARIST

Jesus, my Lord and my God, truly present—Body, Blood, Soul, and Divinity—in the Most Holy Eucharist, I believe in Thy Real Presence.

I love Thee above all things with all my heart, soul, mind, and strength. I thank Thee for giving Thyself and remaining with us in the Most Blessed Sacrament. I worship and adore Thee profoundly.

I wholeheartedly *consecrate* myself entirely to Thee today. I surrender myself completely to Thy goodness and Divine Mercy.

I firmly resolve to prepare to receive Thee in Holy Communion with reverence and love, especially through the practice of the Catholic Faith and frequent reception of the Sacrament of Reconciliation.

I firmly resolve to fulfill my Sunday obligation. Grant me the grace to also frequently receive Thee at Holy Mass on weekdays; and when this is not possible, to at least make a Spiritual Communion. Come now into my heart in Spiritual Holy Communion.

I devote myself to Eucharistic and perpetual adoration. Dear Lord, I pray for the establishment, expansion, and maintenance of adoration in parishes and Christian communities. I firmly resolve to visit and adore Thee often in tabernacles and exposed in monstrances, and to make daily, weekly, or frequent holy hours as my state in life permits.

Help me Lord to be a missionary of the Eucharist by living a Eucharistic life and by inviting others to Mass and adoration, and to embrace the fullness of the true faith.

Mary, Mother of the Eucharist and my mother, Our Lady of the Most Blessed Sacrament, intercede for me with thy Son for the graces to assist devoutly at Holy Mass, communicate worthily, and lovingly visit and adore Jesus in the Most Blessed Sacrament, so that, day by day, my heart may become more like His Eucharistic Heart. Amen.

THE SURRENDER NOVENA

The Surrender Novena was *dictated by Jesus* to Servant of God Don Dolindo Ruotola (October 6, 1882–November 19, 1970), a diocesan priest in Naples, Italy, who was also a Third Order Franciscan and a confessor to St. Padre Pio. Throughout his heroic life, in which he suffered greatly and received the stigmata, Don Dolindo had many conversations with Jesus. He was also very devoted to the Blessed Mother. Padre Pio would tell pilgrims visiting him from Naples that they had their own saint living amongst them, saying that "the whole of paradise was in Don Dolindo's soul."

Jesus gave Don Dolindo the Surrender Novena to share with everyone, especially those suffering from anxiety. In the novena, we surrender ourselves to Jesus and ask Him to take care of everything. Jesus teaches us about total abandonment to God to help console us and lead us in the right direction in our spiritual life.

Praying the novena helps bring peace of soul because we give our anxieties to Jesus with the expectation that He will encourage us not to worry about the consequences of anything. Instead, He calls us into a deeper, more intimate relationship with Himself when we turn to Him for everything and release our control by placing our *complete trust* in Him. He offers us the pure love that flows from His Sacred Heart as we surrender ourselves and our love to Him.

Day 1: Why do you confuse yourselves by worrying? Leave the care of your affairs to Me and everything will be peaceful. I say to you in truth that every act of true, blind, complete surrender to Me produces the effect that you desire and resolves all difficult situations. *Prayer*: O Jesus, I surrender myself to You, take care of everything! (10 times.)

Day 2: Surrender to Me does not mean to fret, worry, and lose hope, nor does it mean offering Me a worried prayer, asking me to follow you and change your worry into prayer. It is against this surrender, deeply against it, to worry, to be nervous, and to desire to think about the results of anything. It is like the confusion that children feel when they ask their mother to see to their needs and then try to take care of those needs for themselves so that their childlike efforts get in their mother's way. Surrender means to placidly close the eyes of the soul, to turn away from thoughts of tribulation, and to put yourself in My care, so that only I act, saying "You take care of it." *Prayer*: O Jesus, I surrender myself to You, take care of everything! (10 times.)

Day 3: How many things I do when the soul, in its spiritual and material needs, turns to Me, looks at Me, and says to Me, "You take care of it," then closes its eyes and rests. In pain, you pray for Me to act, but that I act in the way you desire. You do not turn to Me, instead, you want Me to adapt to your ideas. You are not sick people who ask the doctor to cure you but rather sick people who tell the doctor how to. So do not act this way but pray as I taught you in the Our Father: "Hallowed be Thy Name," that is, be glorified in My need. "Thy kingdom come," that is, let all that is in us and in the world be in accord with Your kingdom. "Thy will be done on Earth as it is in Heaven," that is, in our need, decide as You see fit for our temporal and eternal life. If you say to Me truly: "Thy will be done," which is the same as saying "You take care of it," I will intervene with all My omnipotence, and I will resolve the most difficult situations. *Prayer*: O Jesus, I surrender myself to You, take care of everything! (10 times.)

Day 4: You see evil growing instead of weakening? Do not worry. Close your eyes and say to Me with faith: "Thy will be done, You take care of it." I say to you that I will take care of it, and that I will intervene as does a doctor and I will accomplish miracles when they are needed. Do you see that the sick person is getting worse? Do not be upset, but close your eyes and say, "You take care of it." I say to you that I will take care of it, and that there is no medicine more powerful than My loving intervention. By My love, I promise this to you. *Prayer*: O Jesus, I surrender myself to You, take care of everything! (10 times.)

Day 5: And when I must lead you on a path different from the one you see, I will prepare you; I will carry you in My arms; I will let you find yourself, like children who have fallen asleep in their mother's arms, on the other bank of the river. What troubles you and hurts you immensely are your reason, your thoughts, and your worry, and your desire at all costs to deal with what afflicts you. *Prayer*: O Jesus, I surrender myself to You, take care of everything! (10 times.)

Day 6: You are sleepless; you want to judge everything, direct everything, and see to everything, and you surrender to human strength, or worse—to men themselves, trusting in their intervention. This is what hinders My words and My views. Oh, how much I wish from you this surrender, to help you, and how I suffer when I see you so agitated! Satan tries to do exactly this: to agitate you and to remove you from My protection and to throw you into the jaws of human initiative. So, trust only in Me, rest in Me, surrender to Me in everything. *Prayer*: O Jesus, I surrender myself to You, take care of everything! (10 times.)

Day 7: I perform miracles in proportion to your full surrender to Me and to your not thinking of yourselves. I sow treasure troves of graces when you are in the deepest poverty. No person of reason, no thinker, has ever performed miracles, not even among the saints. He does divine works whosoever surrenders to God. So don't think about it anymore, because your mind is acute and for you it is very hard to see evil and to trust in Me and to not think of yourself. Do this for all your needs, do this, all of you, and you will see great continual silent miracles. I will take care of things. I promise this to you. *Prayer*: O Jesus, I surrender myself to You, take care of everything! (10 times.)

Day 8: Close your eyes and let yourself be carried away on the flowing current of My grace; close your eyes and do not think of the present, turning your thoughts away from the future as you would from temptation. Rest in Me, believing in My goodness, and I promise you by My love that if you say, "You take care of it," I will take care of it completely, I will console you, I will free you, and I will guide you. *Prayer*: O Jesus, I surrender myself to You, take care of everything! (10 times.)

Day 9: Pray always in readiness to surrender, and you will receive from it great peace and great rewards, even when I grant you the grace of immolation, of repentance, and of love. Then what does suffering matter? It seems impossible to you? Close your eyes and say with all your soul, "Jesus, You take care of it." Do not be afraid, I will take care of things, and you will bless My name by humbling yourself. A thousand prayers cannot equal one single act of surrender, remember this well. There is no novena more effective than this. *Prayer*: O Jesus, I surrender myself to You, take care of everything! (10 times.)

THE DEGREES OF THE SPIRITUAL LIFE

[*Note*: The following schema was made by Thomas Verner Moore, a Carthusian (whose name in religion is Pablo Maria), and published as Appendix II (pp. 386–87) to his *The Life of Man with God* (New York: Harcourt Brace, 1956). Dom Moore, a scholar and former professor of psychology and psychiatry at the Catholic University of America, adapted it from Dom Chautard's classic, *The Soul of the Apostolate*.]

1. HARDNESS OF HEART

Mortal Sin: Obstinacy in this sin, by ignorance or a maliciously false conscience. Stifling of remorse or absence of it.

Prayer: Deliberate suppression of all recourse to God.

2. CHRISTIAN ONLY OUTWARDLY

Mortal Sin: Considered as a slight evil, committed on any occasion or temptation.

Prayer: Mechanical, without attention, always dictated by temporal interest.

3. MODERATE PIETY

Mortal Sin: Weak resistance. No flight from occasions, but genuine sorrow and good confession.

Venial Sins: Looked upon as insignificant.

Prayer: Vocal prayers fairly well said, but seldom.

4. INTERMITTENT PIETY

Mortal Sin: Loyal resistance. Habitual avoidance of occasions. Deep regrets. Penance to atone.

Venial Sins: Sometimes deliberate. Weak resistance. Slight regrets.

Prayer: Mental prayer is attempted but often neglected.

5. SUSTAINED PIETY

Mortal Sin: Never, or very rare in a violent, sudden temptation.

Venial Sins: Rarely deliberate. Deeply regretted.

Imperfections: The soul avoids searching for them so as not to be obliged to overcome them.

Prayer: Constant fidelity in spite of everything to daily mental prayer; meditation likely to pass into aspirations of love.

6. FERVOR

Venial Sins: Never deliberate. Slipped into at times through half advertence. Deeply regretted and fervently atoned for.

Imperfections: Guarded against and resisted heartily.

Prayer: Mental prayer willingly prolonged. Often a quiet, silent gazing into the face of God.

7. RELATIVE PERFECTION

Imperfections: Energetically avoided with great love.

Prayer: Habitual life of prayer even while devoting oneself to exterior work. Thirst for self-denial and humiliations. Hunger for the Holy Eucharist and Heaven. Various infused graces of contemplative prayer.

[*Note*: Dom Moore notes that between the Sixth and Seventh degrees "there comes a parting of the ways that unite later on the heights of perfection," the way of extraordinary consolations (e.g., visions, ecstasies, etc.), and the way that is ordinary. The latter way is usually safer and more meritorious.]

POPE LEO XIII ON THE RIGHT ORDERING OF CHRISTIAN LIFE

Excerpts from the Encyclical Letter Exeunte iam anno *(December 25, 1888)*

In the exercise of the high Apostolic office bestowed upon Us by the goodness of God, We have many times, as in duty bound, undertaken the defense of truth, and have striven to expound particularly that teaching which seemed the most opportune for the public welfare, so that, in seeking the truth, all might watchfully and carefully avoid the dangers of error. But now, as a loving parent of his children, We wish to address all Christians, and in simple, homely words to exhort all and each to lead a holy life. For, beyond the mere Profession of Faith, Christian virtues and practices are necessary for the Christian; and upon these depend, not only the eternal salvation of souls, but also the stable peace and true prosperity of the human family and of society.

If we inquire into the kind of life men everywhere lead, it is impossible for anyone to avoid the conclusion that public and private morals differ vastly from the precepts of the Gospel. Too sadly, alas! do the words of the Apostle St. John apply to our age: "All that is in the world is the concupiscence of the flesh, and the concupiscence of the eyes, and the pride of life" (1 Jn 2:16). For in truth most men, with little heed as to whence they have come or whither they are going, place all their thoughts and all their care upon the vain and fleeting goods of this life; and, contrary to nature and right order, they voluntarily give themselves up to serve things of which their reason tells them they should be the masters.

It is a short step from the desire of comfort and luxury to the striving after the means to obtain them. Hence arises the unbridled eagerness to become rich which binds those whom it possesses, and while they are seeking the gratification of their passion, hurries them along, often without reference to justice or injustice, and not infrequently even with insolent contempt for the penury of others. Thus very many who live in luxury call themselves the brethren of the multitudes whom in the depths of their hearts they despise.

With minds puffed up with pride, they strive to be subject to no law and to have respect for no authority. They call self-love liberty and think themselves "born free like a wild ass's colt" (Job 11:12). Snares and temptations to sin abound; impious and immoral dramas are exhibited on the stage; books and the daily press jeer at virtue and ennoble crime; and the fine arts themselves, which were intended for virtuous use and for rightful recreation, are made to minister to depraved passions.

For many nowadays seek to learn truth by the aid of reason alone, putting divine faith entirely aside; and, through the exclusion of this strength and of this light, they fall into many errors and fail to discover the truth. They teach, for instance, that matter alone exists in the world; that men and beasts have the same origin and a like nature; and some even there are who go so far as to doubt the existence of God, the Ruler and Maker of the world, or to err most grievously, like unto the heathen, as to His divine nature.

Hence the very essence and form of virtue, of justice, and of duty are of necessity distorted. Thus it is that, while they hold up to admiration the high authority of reason, and unduly extol the subtlety of the human intellect, they fall into the just punishment of pride through ignorance of what is of the greatest importance. When the mind has thus been poisoned, the moral character becomes at the same time deeply and substantially corrupt; and so diseased a state can be cured only with the utmost difficulty in this class of men, because on the one side their opinions vitiate the judgment of what is right, and on the other they have not the light of Christian faith, which is the principle and foundation of all righteousness.

Daily we see, with our own eyes, as it were, the numerous evils that afflict all classes of men from these causes. Poisonous doctrines have corrupted both public and private life: rationalism, materialism, and atheism have begotten socialism, communism, and nihilism—fatal and pestilential evils, which naturally, and almost necessarily, flow forth from such principles. In good sooth, if the Catholic religion may be rejected with immunity, whose divine origin is made clear by such unmistakable signs, why should not all other forms of religion be rejected, when it is clear that they have not the same evidence of truth?

If the soul is by nature one with the body, and if therefore no hope of a happy eternity remains when the body dies, what reason is there why man should endure toil and suffering here in the endeavor to subject the appetites to right reason? The highest good of man will consist in enjoying the comforts and pleasures of life, and since there is absolutely no one who does not by an instinct and impulse of nature strive after happiness, every man will naturally lay hands on all he can in the hope of living happily on the spoils of others.

Nor will there be any power mighty enough to bridle passions when fully set astir; for if the supreme and eternal law, which commands what is right and forbids what is wrong, be rejected, it follows that the power of law is thwarted, and that all authority is loosened. Hence the bonds of civil society will be utterly shattered, when every man is driven by insatiable greed to a perpetual struggle, some striving to keep what they possess, others to obtain what they covet. Such is more or less the spirit and tone of our age.

There is, nevertheless, some consolation for us, even while looking at existing evils, and we may lift up our heart in good hope. For "God created all things that they might be: and He made the nations of the earth for health" (Wis 1:14). But as all this world cannot be upheld save by the will and providence of Him Who called it out of nothing, so also can men be healed only by the power of Him by Whose goodness they were recalled from death to life. For Jesus Christ redeemed the human race once by the abundant shedding of His Blood; and the efficacy of this great work and gift is for all ages: "Neither is there salvation in any other" (Acts 4:12).

Hence they who strive by the enforcement of law to extinguish the ever-growing flame of popular passions, strive indeed for what is right and just; but they will labor with little or no result so long as they obstinately reject the power of the Gospel and refuse the assistance of the Church. These evils can be cured only by a change of principles, and by *returning in public and private conduct to Jesus Christ and to a Christian Rule of Life.*

Now the whole essence of a Christian life is not to take part in the corruption of the world, but to oppose constantly any indulgence in that corruption. This is taught by all the words and actions, by all the laws and institutions, by the very life and death of Jesus Christ, "the author and finisher of faith" (Heb 12:2).

Hence, however strongly we are drawn back by our evil nature and the profligacy that is around us, it is our duty to run to the "fight proposed to us" (Heb 12:1), armed and prepared with the same courage and the same weapons as He Who, "having joy set before Him, endured the cross" (Heb 12:2). Wherefore men are bound to consider and understand this above all, that it is contrary to the profession and duty of a Christian to follow, as they are wont to do, every kind of pleasure, to shrink from the hardship attending a virtuous life, and to allow oneself all that gratifies and delights the senses. "They that are Christ's have crucified their flesh with the vices and concupiscences" (Gal 5:24).

Hence it follows that they who are not accustomed to suffer, and to disregard ease and pleasure, belong not to Christ. By the infinite goodness of God, man was restored to the hope of an immortal life from which he had been cut off; but he cannot attain to it if he strives not to walk in the very footsteps of Christ, and to conform his mind and life to that of Christ by meditating on His example. Therefore, this is not a counsel, but a duty; and the duty, not only of those who desire a more perfect life, but of all — "always bearing about in our body the mortification of Jesus" (2 Cor 4:10).

How else shall the natural law, which commands man to live virtuously, be kept? For by holy baptism the sin which we contracted at birth is taken away, but the evil and perverse roots which it has planted in our hearts are by no means removed. That part of man which is without reason, although harmless to those who fight manfully by the grace of Christ, nevertheless struggles with reason for supremacy, disturbs the whole soul, and tyrannically bends the will away from virtue with such power that we cannot escape vice or do our duty *except by a daily struggle.*

The Council of Trent says: "This holy synod teaches that in the baptized there remains concupiscence or an inclination to evil, which, being left to be fought against, cannot hurt those who, instead of yielding to it, manfully fight against it by the grace of Jesus Christ; for he who hath lawfully striven shall be crowned" (Sess. V, can. 5). There is in this struggle a degree of valor to which only a very perfect virtue attains, such as belongs to those who, by putting to flight impulses opposed to right reason, have made such advances in virtue as to seem almost to live a heavenly life on earth.

Granted that few attain excellence so great, yet even the philosophy of the ancients taught that every man should conquer his evil desires; and still more and with greater care should those do so who, from daily contact with the world are more sorely tempted—unless it be foolishly thought that where the danger is, greater watchfulness is less needed, or that they whose maladies are most grievous need medicine more seldom.

But the toil which has to be borne in this conflict is compensated by great blessings over and above its eternal reward in Heaven; and particularly because by the quelling of the passions, nature is in a measure restored to its original dignity. For man has been born under a law that the soul should rule the body, and that the appetites should be restrained by mind and reason; and hence it follows that to restrain evil passions striving for the mastery over us is our noblest and greatest freedom. Moreover, it is difficult to see what can be expected of a man, even as a member of society, who is not thus disposed. Will anyone be inclined to do right who has been accustomed to make self-love the sole rule of what he should do or avoid doing? No man can be high-souled, or kind, or merciful, or restrained who has not learned to conquer self, and to despise all worldly things when opposed to virtue.

Nor must We refrain from affirming that it seems to have been determined in the designs of God that there should be no salvation for men without struggle and pain. Indeed, when God gave to man pardon for sin, He gave it under the condition that His only begotten Son would pay its just and due penalty; and though Jesus Christ might have satisfied divine justice in other ways, nevertheless He preferred to satisfy it by the utmost suffering and the sacrifice of His life.

Therefore, He has imposed it upon His followers as a law signed with His Blood that their life should be an endless strife with the vices of their age.

What made the Apostles unconquerable in their mission of teaching truth to the world? What strengthened our countless Martyrs in bearing witness by their blood to the Christian faith? Their more than readiness to obey fearlessly this law. All who have taken heed to live a Christian life and to seek after virtue have trodden the same path. We, too, must walk along this road if we desire to assure either our own salvation or that of others.

Therefore, in the unbounded license that prevails, it is necessary for everyone to guard manfully against the allurements of luxury; and since on every side there is so much pretentious display of enjoyment in wealth, the soul must be strengthened against the dangerous share of wealth, lest, in striving after what are called the good things of life, which cannot satisfy and soon fade away, the soul should lose "the treasure in Heaven which faileth not" (Lk 12:33).

Finally, it is a further matter of deep grief that free thought and evil example have had such an influence in enfeebling the minds of men as to make many ashamed of the name of Christian—a shame which is the sign either of hopeless wickedness or of extreme cowardice. Each of these is detestable, and each injurious in the extreme. For what salvation remains for men, or on what hope can they rely, if they cease to glory in the name of Jesus Christ, if they openly and constantly refuse to live by the precepts of the Gospel?

It is a common complaint that the age is barren of courageous men. *Bring back into vogue a Christian Rule of Life and the minds of men will forthwith regain their strength and constancy.*

But man's power of itself is not equal to the responsibility of so many and such various duties. As we must ask of God our daily bread for the sustenance of the body, so must we pray to Him for strength of soul that we may be sustained in virtue. Hence that universal condition and law of our life, which We have said is a perpetual warfare, brings with it the necessity of prayer to God. For, as is well and gracefully said by St. Augustine, devout prayer passes beyond the world's space and calls down the mercy of God from Heaven.

In order to conquer the assaults of our passions and the snares of the devil, lest we be led into evil, we are commanded to seek the divine help in the words: "Pray that ye enter not into temptation" (Mt 26:41). How much more is this necessary if we wish to labor profitably for the salvation of others also!

Christ Our Lord, the only-begotten Son of God, the source of all grace and virtue, first showed by example what He taught in word: "He passed the whole night in the prayer of God" (Lk 6:12); and when nigh to the sacrifice of His life, "He prayed the longer" (Lk 22:43). The frailty of nature would be much less perilous, and the moral character less weak and languid, if that divine precept of prayer were not so much disregarded and treated almost with dislike. God is easily appeased, He desires to do good to men, having clearly promised to give His grace in abundance to those who ask for it. Nay, He even invites men to ask, and almost insists upon their asking, with most loving words: "I say unto you, ask, and it shall be given to you; seek and you shall find; knock and it shall be opened unto you" (Lk 11:9).

And that we may have no fear in doing this with all confidence and familiarity, He makes use of tender phrases, comparing Himself to a most loving father who desires nothing so much as the love of his children: "If you then, being evil, know how to give good gifts to your children, how much more will your Father, who is in Heaven, give good things to them that ask Him" (Mt 7:11).

Whoever considers these things will not wonder at the efficacy of human prayer seeming so great to St. John Chrysostom that he thought it might be compared with the divine power. For, as God created all things by His word, so man by prayer obtains whatever he wills. *Nothing has so great a power to obtain grace for us as prayer when rightly made*; for it contains the motives by which God easily allows Himself to be appeased and to incline to mercy.

In prayer we separate ourselves from things of earth; filled with the thought of God alone, we become conscious of our human weakness and therefore, resting in the goodness and embrace of our Heavenly Father, we seek refuge in the power of Him Who created us. We approach the Author of all good as if pressing Him to look upon our weak souls, unsteadfast strength, and great poverty; and, full of hope, we implore His aid and guardianship, Who alone can heal our infirmities, and give help to us in our weakness and misery. By such a condition of mind, in which, as is fitting, we think humbly of ourselves, God is greatly moved to mercy, for "God resisteth the proud, but to the humble He giveth grace" (1 Pet 5:5).

Let, then, the habit of prayer be sacred to all; let the mind and heart and voice pray together; and let our life be in conformity with our prayer, so that by keeping the divine laws, the course of our days may seem a continual ascent towards God.

The virtue of prayer of which we are speaking is, like other virtues, produced and nourished by divine faith. For God is the author of all true and alone desirable blessings. To Him also we owe our knowledge of His infinite goodness, and of the merits of Jesus our Redeemer. But, on the other hand, *nothing is more fitted for the nourishment and increase of faith than the pious habit of prayer.*

RECOMMENDED SPIRITUAL READING: THE CLASSICS

[*Note*: The following recommendations that Fr. Bradley prepared for a graduate school class he taught on the Rule of Life for the Laity is not meant to be a list of "the seventeen best books" in spirituality, although many of the titles included here would very probably be on such a list if it were compiled. What he intended here is simply a manageable number of books in English, currently in print and readily available in inexpensive editions from various publishers. Arranged chronologically, this list suggests something of the scope and depth of Catholic spiritual thought and thus provides the reader with an excellent occasion to grow in wisdom and grace.]

THE HOLY BIBLE, in a Catholic Edition, especially the New Testament

This book is absolutely unique, for it is literally the Word of God. Reading in it, and particularly in the four Gospels, should come before—and after—any and all other reading.

LITURGY OF THE HOURS, also known as The Divine Office

This is the prayer of the Church. It is in four volumes and is prayed daily by priests and deacons, as well as members of religious congregations and third orders. It can be purchased in condensed form as one volume for members of the laity who want to pray with it.

ST. AUGUSTINE, *Confessions*

Perhaps this is the most famous and influential contribution, after the Scriptures themselves, to both the content and the form of all spiritual writing that is genuinely Catholic.

ST. CATHERINE OF SIENA, *The Dialogues*

This book is one of the most striking manifestations of grace in all history—the relaying to us of Christ's own words via an illiterate mystic, who is now honored and invoked as a Doctor of the Church.

THOMAS À KEMPIS, *The Imitation of Christ*

This is possibly the most important single work in the entire history of Christian spirituality. It is all the more important for our time because of its relative neglect, which surely explains in part the low spiritual ebb of the "contemporary Church."

ST. IGNATIUS LOYOLA, *Spiritual Exercises*

Unlike the other books on this list, this one is less to be "read" than to be "done," i.e., it is but a set of instructions for making a retreat. Yet, its very words are a sacramental, undoubtedly one of God's most tested and special instruments for the constant renewal of His Church.

ST. TERESA OF AVILA, *The Way of Perfection*

A perfect treatise on the ways of prayer by one whom the Church has officially recognized as perhaps her pre-eminent Doctor in this area of the Christian life. Although written for cloistered nuns and touching on the high mysteries of infused prayer, the doctrine of this extraordinarily sensible and practical woman (as evidenced even more clearly in her magnificent *Autobiography*) is perfectly applicable to all. Also recommended is St. Theresa's *Interior Castle*.

ST. FRANCIS DE SALES, *Introduction to the Devout Life*

One of the greatest of all spiritual classics, this little book marked the beginning, in its truest sense, of the "Age of the Laity" in the Church. Its doctrine is a perfect blend of the traditional wisdom of the saints and its application to a situation that is essentially contemporary and actually lived by the vast majority of Christians.

ST. JANE FRANCES DE CHANTAL, *On Prayer*

A collection of very brief and concise counsels on the value and the art of prayer, by a saint who combined in her life the vocations of wife, mother, widow, and religious.

ST. LOUIS-MARIE GRIGNON DE MONTFORT, *True Devotion to the Blessed Virgin*

A classic combination of devout theology and theological devotion that deservedly has had as much effect on the spiritual vitality of Christians as any other book one can think of.

ST. ALPHONSUS MARIA DE LIGUORI, *Prayer, the Great Means of Salvation and Perfection*

The graces necessary for salvation cannot be obtained from God except by prayer, explains the legendary eighteenth-century saint and Doctor of the Church. This book is one of the most powerful and accessible primers on the art of prayer ever written. Also recommended is his magnificent book, *Uniformity with God's Will*, in which he taught that the more one unites his will with the divine will, the greater will be his love of God—challenging and encouraging.

ST. THÉRÈSE OF LISIEUX, *Autobiography*

A treasury of wisdom and simplicity bequeathed to all "little souls" by the "greatest saint of our time." Her doctrine is a kind of condensation of all that had preceded her, conformably to that original matrix that is the Gospel itself. This book is a "short-cut," surely, for this confused and feverish world of our time.

DOM JEAN-BAPTISTE CHAUTARD, O.C.S.O., *The Soul of the Apostolate*

This little book, first published with the approbation and blessing of Pope St. Pius X, has undoubtedly been the source of immense good in the Church. Its basic thesis, that prayer is "the soul of the apostolate," is clearly the most important lesson for the true renewal of the Church today.

DIETRICH VON HILDEBRAND, *Transformation in Christ*

Published in 1940, this is one of the greatest spiritual writings of the Twentieth Century, by one of the Church's greatest lights. It is a magnificent development of the distinctive Hildebrandian theme of the Sacred Humanity of Christ.

DOM EUGENE BOYLAN, O.C.R., *This Tremendous Lover*

Dom Boylan, a Trappist, explains God's plan for our happiness and how we are each called to participate in this divine plan as members of the Mystical Body of Christ.

MONSIGNOR ROMANO GUARDINI, *Prayer in Practice*

An excellent study of prayer in most of its aspects, by a

great contemporary scholar, published in 1957. It is at once profoundly orthodox and brilliantly original. Guardini's greatest work, *The Lord*, as indeed any of his works, is also highly recommended.

PÈRE JEAN DU CŒUR DE JÉSUS D'ELBÉE, *I Believe in Love*

This is a superb little treatise on the Theresian doctrine of "the Little Way," and thus a perfect summation of the needs, personal and apostolic, and their corresponding resources, for the Catholics of our time — and always.

RECOMMENDED CONTEMPORARY AND CLASSIC BOOKS

[*Note*: As you journey to living within the Sacred Heart of Jesus and formulate your personal Rule of Life, there are several contemporary books available from Catholic publishers to help you on your way. A selection supplementing the original bibliography prepared by Fr. Bradley is listed here to correspond to the chapters in the book. More information about each book can be found on the publishers' websites.]

THE HOLY EUCHARIST

Calloway, Fr. Donald M., M.I.C. *Eucharistic Gems: Daily Wisdom on the Blessed Sacrament*. Stockbridge, MA: Marian Press, 2023.

Eymard, St. Peter Julian. *The Real Presence*. Edmond, OK: Veritatis Splendor Publications, 2013.

———. *How to Get More Out of Holy Communion*. Manchester, NH: Sophia Institute Press, 2000.

Frances of Rome, St. (translated by Fr. Robert Nixon, O.S.B.). *The Eucharistic Visions of St. Frances of Rome*. Manchester, NH: Sophia Institute Press, 2024.

Institute of St. Clement I, Pope and Martyr. *The Eucharistic Miracles of the World*. Bardstown, KY: Eternal Life Publishing, 2016.

International Society of the Eucharist, The. *33 Days to Eucharistic Glory*. North Palm Beach, FL: Blue Sparrow Books, 2023.

Maingot, Fr. Jesse J., O.P., and Fr. Ignatius John Schweitzer. *How to Be His: A 33-Day Dedication to Our Eucharistic Jesus*. Manchester, NH: Sophia Institute Press, 2025.

Mectilde de Bar, Mother (foreword by Dom Mark Kirby, O.S.B.). *The Mystery of Incomprehensible Love: The Eucharistic Message of Mother Mectilde of the Blessed Sacrament*. Brooklyn, NY: Angelico Press, 2020.

O'Connor, Rev. James T. *The Hidden Manna: A Theology of the Eucharist*. San Francisco, CA: Ignatius Press, 1988.

Stice, Fr. Randy L. *Eucharistic Amazement: Experience the Wonder of the Mass*. Boston, MA: Pauline Books & Media, 2025.

EUCHARISTIC ADORATION

Beckman, Kathleen. *Rekindle Eucharistic Amazement*. Goleta, CA: Queenship Publishing, 2008.

Groeschel, Fr. Benedict J., C.F.R., and James Monti. *In the Presence of Our Lord: The History, Theology, and Psychology of Eucharistic Devotion*. Huntington, IN: Our Sunday Visitor, 1997.

Guernsey, Daniel P. *Adoration: Eucharistic Texts and Prayers Throughout Church History*. San Francisco: Ignatius Press, 1999.

THE SACRED HEART OF JESUS

Arnoudt, Rev. Peter J., S.J. *Imitation of the Sacred Heart of Jesus*. Charlotte, NC: TAN Books, 2011.

Beckman, Kathleen. *Beautiful Holiness: A Spiritual Journey with Blessed Conchita to the Heart of Jesus*. Manchester, NH: Sophia Institute Press, 2022.

A Benedictine Monk. *In Sinu Jesu: When Heart Speaks to Heart: A Journal of a Priest at Prayer*. Brooklyn, NY: Angelico Press, 2016.

Croiset, Fr. John, S.J. *Devotion to the Sacred Heart of Jesus*. Hanover, PA: American Society for the Defense of Tradition, Family and Property, 2020.

Dailey, Fr. Thomas, O.S.F.S. *Behold This Heart: St. Francis de Sales and Devotion to the Sacred Heart*. Manchester, NH: Sophia Institute Press, 2021.

Gaitley, Fr. Michael, M.I.C. *Consoling the Heart of Jesus: A Do-It-Yourself Retreat*. Stockbridge, MA: Marian Press, 2009 (also has a Study Guide).

Larkin, Rev. Francis, SS.C.C. *Enthronement of the Sacred Heart*. Boston, MA: Daughters of St. Paul, 1978.

Leo XIII, Pope, and Pope Pius XI. *Catholic Papal Writings on the Sacred Heart of Jesus*. Potosi, WI: St. Athanasius Press, 2016.

O'Donnell, Timothy T. *Heart of the Redeemer*. San Francisco, CA: Ignatius Press, 2017.

Poor Clare Nuns of St. Joseph Monastery, The. *Manual for Eucharistic Adoration*. Charlotte, NC: TAN Books, 2016.

Serratelli, Most Rev. Arthur J. *Eucharistic Adoration: Scriptural Reflections and Prayers*. Totowa, NJ: Catholic Book Publishing Corporation, 2021.

Udell, Stefan. *Word Made Flesh: Meditations of the Saints on the Sacred Heart*. Brooklyn, NY: Angelico Press, 2025.

INTERIOR LIFE

Bradley, Fr. Robert Ignatius, S.J. *Our Lady's Psalter: Reflections on the Mysteries of the Traditional Rosary*. Brooklyn, NY: Angelico Press, 2025.

Burke, Dan. *The Devil in the Castle: St. Teresa of Avila, Spiritual Warfare, and the* Progress *of the Soul*. Manchester, NH: Sophia Institute Press, 2021.

Burke, Dan, with Fr. John Bartunek, L.C. *Navigating the Interior Life: Spiritual Direction and the Journey to God*. Manchester, NH: Sophia Institute Press, 2012.

Calloway, Fr. Donald H., M.I.C. *Consecration to St. Joseph: The Wonders of Our Spiritual Father.* Stockbridge, MA: Marian Press, 2020.

Cameron, Fr. Peter John, O.P. *Praying with St. Paul: Daily Reflections on the Letters of the Apostle Paul.* Yonkers, NY: Magnificat, 2008.

Doyle, Msgr. Charles Hugo, *Guidance in Spiritual Direction: Advice from the Holiest Men and Women of All Time*. Manchester, NH: Sophia Institute Press, 2023.

Gallagher, Timothy M., O.M.V. *The Discernment of Spirits: An Ignatian Guide for Everyday Living*. New York, NY: The Crossroad Publishing Company, 2005 (there is a Study Guide to accompany this book).

Galot, Fr. Jean, S.J. *Seven Ways of the Cross*. Brooklyn, NY: Angelico Press, 2024.

Hardon, Fr. John A., S.J. *Theology of Prayer*. Boston, MA: Daughters of St. Paul, 1979.

Hollcraft, Joseph. *Unleashing the Power of Intercessory Prayer*. Manchester, NH: Sophia Institute Press, 2020.

Kapler, Shane. *Through, With & In Him: The Prayer Life of Jesus and How To Make It Our Own*. Brooklyn, NY: Angelico Press, 2014.

Khoury, Jean. *Praying with the Heart: The Little Way to Jesus*. Brooklyn, NY: Angelico Press, 2015.

Kirby, Fr. Jeffrey. *Lord Teach Us to Pray: A Guide to the Spiritual*

Life and Christian Discipleship. Gastonia, NC: St. Benedict Press, 2014.

Lehodey, Rt. Rev. Dom Vitalis, O.C.R. *The Ways of Mental Prayer*. Charlotte, NC: TAN Books, 2012.

Marmion, Blessed Columba. *Our Way and Our Life: Christ in His Mysteries*. Brooklyn, NY: Angelico Press, 2013.

———. *Christ the Life of the Soul*. Brooklyn, NY: Angelico Press, 2012.

Mother Angelica. *Mother Angelica's Keys to the Interior Life*. Irondale, AL: EWTN Publishing, 2024.

———. *Mother Angelica's Guide to the Spiritual* Life. Irondale, AL: EWTN Publishing, 2021.

Nichols, Fr. Aidan, O.P. *A Spirituality for the Twenty-First Century*. Huntington, IN: Our Sunday Visitor Publishing, 2003.

Sattler, Fr. Wayne. *Remain in Me and I in You: Relating to God as a Person, Not an Idea*. Manchester, NH: Sophia Institute Press, 2025.

Sheen, Bishop Fulton J. *Go to Heaven: A Spiritual Road Map to Eternity*. San Francisco, CA: Ignatius Press, 2017.

Thibaut, Raymond (editor). *Union with God According to the Letters of Dom Marmion*. Brooklyn, NY: Angelico Press, 2022.

SALVIFIC SUFFERING

Beckman, Kathleen. *Praying the Passion of the Christ: Uniting Your Suffering to His*. Goleta, CA: Queenship Publishing, 2004.

Emmerich, Blessed Anne Catherine. *The Dolorous Passion of Our Lord Jesus Christ*. Charlotte, NC: TAN Books, 1983.

Giszczak, Mark. *Suffering: What Every Catholic Should Know*. Greenwood Village, CO: Augustine Institute, 2024.

Hjelmstad, Megan. *Offer It Up: Discovering the Power and Purpose of Redemptive Suffering*. Steubenville, OH: Emmaus Road Publishing, 2025.

Mahar, Fr. Christopher M. *Finding God in Suffering*. Boston, MA: Pauline Books & Media, 2023.

Mihalik, Paul A., O.C.D.S. *Offering of Suffering*. Goleta, CA: Queenship Publishing Company, 2000.

Mother Angelica. *On Suffering and Burnout*. Irondale, AL: EWTN Publishing, Inc., 2016.

Van Zeller, Hubert. *Suffering with a Purpose: How to Turn Failures into Victories and Pain into Joy*. Manchester, NH: The Heritage Press, 2002.

RULE OF LIFE

Barry, Patrick, Richard Yeo, and Kathleen Norris. *Wisdom from the Monastery: The Rule of St. Benedict for Everyday Life*. Collegeville, MN: Liturgical Press, 2006.

Beckman, Kathleen. *Praying for Priests: An Urgent Call for the Salvation of Souls*. Manchester, NH: Sophia Institute Press, 2018.

———. *God's Healing Mercy: Finding Your Path to Forgiveness, Peace and Joy*. Manchester, NH: Sophia Institute Press, 2015.

Burke, Dan. *Finding Peace in the Storm: Reflections on St. Alphonsus Liguori's Uniformity with God's Will*. Manchester, NH: Sophia Institute Press, 2023.

Cameli, Louis J. *The Devil You Don't Know: Recognizing and Resisting Evil in Everyday Life*. Notre Dame, IN: Ave Maria Press, 2011.

Gallagher, Timothy, O.M.V. *Struggles in the Spiritual Life: Their Nature and Their Remedies*. Manchester, NH: Sophia Institute Press, 2022.

Groeschel, Fr. Benedict J., C.F.R. *The Virtue Driven Life*. Huntington, IN: Our Sunday Visitor, 2006.

Haase, Albert, O.F.M. *This Sacred Moment: Becoming Holy Right Where You Are*. Downer's Grove, IL: Intervarsity Press, 2010.

Kirby, Fr. Jeffrey. *Kingdom of Happiness: Living the Beatitudes in Everyday Life*. Gastonia, NC: St. Benedict Press, 2017.

———. *Real Discipleship*. Gastonia, NC: St. Benedict Press, 2024.

Schryvers, Fr. Joseph, C.S.S.R. *The Gift of Oneself: Surrendering Oneself to God as a Way of Life*. Charlotte, NC: TAN Books, 2006.

Sheen, Bishop Fulton J. *The Cross and the Beatitudes*. Brooklyn, NY: Angelico Press, 2012.

Strickland, Bishop Joseph E. *Light and Leaven: The Challenge of the Laity in the Twenty-First Century*. El Cajon, CA: Catholic Answers Press, 2020.

ABOUT THE AUTHOR

FATHER ROBERT IGNATIUS BRADLEY, S.J., born on May 15, 1924, began his long journey to the priesthood at the age of three, when he asked his parents, Joseph and Muriel Bradley of Spokane, WA, to give him everything he needed to "celebrate Mass" as his birthday present. His father's friend, a woodworker, carved an eight-inch tall chalice and a paten and painted them gold, while the mother of newly-appointed Spokane Bishop Charles D. White sewed the altar cloth and vestments, making them a little large so he could grow into them. His mother baked "communion hosts" and provided grape juice, altar candles, and a Missal.

And so, on May 15, 1927, with two older brothers drafted as altar boys, the large family and friends, and Bishop White and his mother, gathered in makeshift pews, the future Fr. Bradley solemnly "celebrated" his first "Mass" in Latin. According to family legend, the sermon was targeted at the misdeeds of his four older brothers and lasted quite a long time. The chalice and paten still remain as a family treasure.

As he progressed through St. Augustine School and Gonzaga High School, Fr. Bradley shared duties with his brothers as altar boys for Bishop White's daily Masses at his residence. Two weeks after graduating from Gonzaga in 1941, he followed his older brother Richard into the Society of Jesus. On August 15, 1955, Fr. Bradley was ordained to the priesthood in Louvain, Belgium, beginning his journey first as a priest serving the people of God but also as a renowned scholar and professor in the Jesuit tradition.

The Oregon Province of the Society of Jesus sent him to Columbia University to study for a doctorate in history and then assigned him to teach history at Seattle University. He was promoted to dean of the College of Arts and Sciences but found administrative work unsuitable. He wanted to be in the classroom, and so upon the invitation of Fr. John Hardon, S.J., he joined the faculty of a new catechetical institute at

St. John's University in New York, where he taught theology.

While at St. John's, Fr. Bradley became the chaplain of a new organization founded in the wake of Vatican Council II, Catholics United for the Faith. He served CUF for thirty-five years, writing many articles for *Lay Witness Magazine*, conducting retreats and providing spiritual guidance. He also wrote many articles and book reviews for *Homiletic and Pastoral Review* and contributed chapters to the new Catholic Encyclopedia and several books on theology and catechetics.

In 1983, Father joined the faculty of the Notre Dame Pontifical Catechetical Institute in Arlington, VA, now the Notre Dame Graduate School of Christendom College in Front Royal, VA. He taught many courses in theology to graduate students as well as candidates for the diaconate in the Diocese of Arlington.

A sabbatical took Fr. Bradley to Rome in the mid-1980s to work on a Doctorate in Sacred Theology (S. T. D.) at the Pontifical University of St. Thomas Aquinas (the Angelicum), which he received in 1988. Upon resuming his duties at the Notre Dame Institute, he also became the chaplain for the Poor Clare Monastery in Alexandria, VA, serving the sisters for ten years.

Not one to ever be idle, Father co-authored a translation of *The Roman Catechism* (Pauline Books and Media, 1986) with Monsignor Eugene Kevane, lectured at conferences on the Rosary and the Blessed Mother, conducted retreats, and served as chaplain for the Legion of Mary in Northern Virginia. During the summers, he was the director of Our Lady of Peace Catechetical Institute in Beaverton, OR. Fr. Bradley also authored *The Roman Catechism in the Catechetical Tradition of the Church* (Rowman & Littlefield, 1990).

He moved to his mother's home state of Texas in 1996, where he accepted an adjunct faculty position in theology at the University of Dallas Institute for Religious and Pastoral Studies and also served as adjunct faculty at Our Lady of Guadalupe Seminary of the Fraternal Society of St. Peter (F. S. S. P.) in Denton, NE. Assigned by the bishop of Austin to pastoral work, Fr. Bradley was the celebrant for the weekly liturgies of the St. Joseph Latin Mass Society at St. Mary Cathedral, until he became ill in late 2011. He also served as chaplain to the Legion of Mary in Austin, offered lectures in theology for the laity, and worked individually with students from the University of Texas-Austin who wished to enter the Catholic Church.

On December 20, 2013, Fr. Bradley went home to God. He is buried in the Jesuit Cemetery in Spokane near his older brother Fr. Richard S. Bradley, S. J.

www.ingramcontent.com/pod-product-compliance
Lightning Source LLC
LaVergne TN
LVHW090604110826
845146LV00001B/250

* 9 7 9 8 8 9 2 8 0 1 9 5 9 *